Without A VOICE

SHEA RAMSDELL

BALBOA.PRESS
A DIVISION OF HAY HOUSE

Copyright © 2021 Shea Ramsdell.

All rights reserved. No part of this book may be used or reproduced by any means, graphic, electronic, or mechanical, including photocopying, recording, taping or by any information storage retrieval system without the written permission of the author except in the case of brief quotations embodied in critical articles and reviews.

Balboa Press books may be ordered through booksellers or by contacting:

Balboa Press
A Division of Hay House
1663 Liberty Drive
Bloomington, IN 47403
www.balboapress.com
844-682-1282

Because of the dynamic nature of the Internet, any web addresses or links contained in this book may have changed since publication and may no longer be valid. The views expressed in this work are solely those of the author and do not necessarily reflect the views of the publisher, and the publisher hereby disclaims any responsibility for them.

The author of this book does not dispense medical advice or prescribe the use of any technique as a form of treatment for physical, emotional, or medical problems without the advice of a physician, either directly or indirectly. The intent of the author is only to offer information of a general nature to help you in your quest for emotional and spiritual well-being. In the event you use any of the information in this book for yourself, which is your constitutional right, the author and the publisher assume no responsibility for your actions.

Any people depicted in stock imagery provided by Getty Images are models, and such images are being used for illustrative purposes only. Certain stock imagery © Getty Images.

Print information available on the last page.

ISBN: 978-1-9822-7237-1 (sc)
ISBN: 978-1-9822-7238-8 (e)

Balboa Press rev. date: 08/10/2021

Trauma comes in many forms, and the affects it has on one's life can be devastating. Some recover from the events, yet many cannot overcome the trauma. The man depicted here spent half of his life feeling alone, misunderstood by everyone he contacted. Unable to convey his thoughts or feelings to anyone. The events that occurred during his childhood profoundly impacted his life and others. This is his story, the decline, and the rise of how he overcame the odds of living everyday life. It was his undying love of one person in his life that motivated him to so. This is for her.

Contents

Chapter 1

Family	1
Fear	3
Goodbye	8
Good Times	11
Downward Spiral	15
Sickness	20
Falling Into Despair	24
Spiral Continues	28
An Upward Trend	31
School Issues	34
Things Are Looking Up	36
Building Confidence	38
Finding His Way	42
Awkward Moments	45
Having Fun	47

Chapter 2

A New Journey	55
Coming Into His Own	56
Memorable Moments	60
Slipping Into A Dark Place	63
A Fresh Start	66
Falling Down	68
A New Love	70

An Upward Trend 74
Memorable Year 76
Tension's Building 78
A Time of Change 80
The Love of His Life 82
Tension's Mount 85
Time's with his Daughter 88
Holding on 91
End of The Relationship 93

Chapter 3

Mounting Turmoil 99
Season of Change 102
Growing Pains 103
Change 106
Awkward Moments 108
The Accident 109
Loss and Heartache 110
Feeling like a Failure 114
His Daughter's Dilemma's 115
The Tunnel Deepens 117
The Journey South 123
Walking through Hell and Back 134
Moving forward 138

CHAPTER 1

Family

Thomas, a blue-eyed, blonde-haired boy, had a childhood like any other boy growing up during the 1970s in the suburbs of Sheboygan. Between the four seasons and living along Lake Michigan, it made it one of Michigan's most pristine places. The Suburbs were peaceful, away from all hustle and bustle of big city life. Low crime and low pollution. Everyone could leave their doors and windows open and unlocked during the summer months. Filling the house with the sounds of crickets, frogs, and the occasional sound of the train making its way along the lakes between the major cities.

His parents grew up in the area, as well as his grandparents. His paternal grandparents lived an normal life. His grandfather was a stout man and was a WWII vet who was part of the liberation of the France during the war. After the war, he worked in sales at a chain store and continued to serve in the military, later retiring as a (CMSgt) E-9 Chief Master Sergeant. The local barber, who also served in the military with him, told him a story about his grandfather later in life. How he would have a cigarette pursed between his lips with the majority of it being ash. Talking and going through a file cabinet and not a bit of the ash dropping. Once he retired and they were cleaning out that same file cabinet that was loaded with ash. His grandmother was smaller, standing at 5' and was a registered nurse who went through a local nursing school. Like everyone else in those times, she also smoked, later becoming asthmatic and suffering from emphysema. They had two boys, Thomas's father being the oldest.

His maternal grandparents were not as fortunate in their lives. His grandfather whom Thomas thought looked like Popeye, served in the military as an Electricians' mate. He rarely spoke of his time during the war. But when he did, he would be drinking cans of Pabst Blue Ribbon, and with a squint in one eye, he would exclaim, "I sailed the Seven Seas, if ya don't believe me ask my boys." It is known that he was in some major battles and even survived a sinking ship. After the war, he worked for a local company doing electrical work. His grandmother, a heavyset woman, worked various jobs in her life. Her father left her mother at a young age. A few years later, her mother passed away from tuberculosis, leaving her an orphan, and her aunt took her in to be raised. They had four children and lived in a small house sleeping in the basement. His grandfather had rigged a buzzer with an intercom that would ring in the kitchen. He would ask his wife for various things, and she would oblige. Thomas's mother was the oldest of the two girls who slept in one room, while the two boys slept in another. Little did he know how much of an impact they would have on his life during his childhood years.

Thomas's father who stood at 5'1, was born after the war and graduated during the mid-1960s. After graduation he became employed at the local gas station and later at the local hospital, working in the kitchen. His mother worked at a local manufacturing plant. It was not the best of jobs but it helped pay the bills but their salaries combined, they lived a comfortable life. Thomas's mother often talked of how they met and that when they married, she was treated like a princess by his side of the family. How his father was a gentleman and asked her father for her hand in marriage. A fairy tale wedding in her eyes. It was a story Thomas often heard when he was young, something he wanted when he grew older. His sister, his only other sibling, is two years older than he was, and we were never close. Not finding out until years later the reason why.

Fear

The four seasons were a blessing yet a curse for Thomas. He was very sick as a child, and it was mainly during the winter months when he was at his worst. Being asthmatic and having high temperatures that led to seizures kept him home and indoors. Unable to go out and partake in regular childhood activities like sledding and snowball fights. The summer month's made up that, though, allowing him to run and play as an average child would.

Some of his earliest memories were that of fear, that of the unknown. People around Thomas were overprotective, using fear as a way to control. During the summer months, kids would swim near the old oil docks. His mother would warn him to stay away from that area because of how dangerous it was. How he could drown because of the turbulent water in that area. That did not stop him from exploring the area with his childhood friend. His friend lived a block away and was the same age as Thomas. They walked to the site, and he remembers it being overgrown with trees and brush. He wanted to walk out on the wooden remains of the dock's but Thomas wouldn't. The words his mother spoke echoing in his mind. That was the first time being teased for not wanting to do something. His mother often told Thomas and his sister how things worked when she was a child. How she would have to pick a switch or get hit with a belt from her father. When they returned home and spoke of where they were when she asked, the words flew out of her mouth. "Wait till your father gets home; he is going to get the belt out." And sure enough, when he came home, he came upstairs with a belt in hand. But he did not use it. Those words and that image were forever engraved in his mind as that scenario played out in the coming years. A belt was never used, but he was spanked accordingly.

He was always an early riser, and sometimes he would sit in his room and play with the fan and the electrical cord. While putting his hand close to the fan, his finger went inside, causing it to stop. It scared him, of course, and other times he would play with the electrical cord, unplugging and plugging it back in with the fan still running. Getting the occasional shock that didn't frighten him as he continued to try and get that same feeling back that coursed through his body.

There was a girl with who he hung out around this time. She was a tomboy. Thinking back, she reminded him of Velma from Scooby-Doo. She wore glasses with an eye patch covering one eye. They had so much fun together. Building forts with the blanket's in his living room and laying underneath talking about who knows what. Laying out in the grass and staring up into the blue sky. She was not around long as she was visiting her grandmother. His only other memory is seeing her one more time without the eye patch and then never again. He often thought about her over the years and wondered what became of her.

Around this same time, Thomas and his friends went to the local park to play. Thomas wanted to climb up on the monkey bars. Looking back at that time, the monkey bars seemed as large as the cage Mad Max was in during the movie Beyond Thunder Dome. All the neighborhood kids were at the top, and Thomas was determined to climb to be there also. He made it a quarter away from the top and froze. Thomas could not move an inch as tears filled his eyes. The kids at the top began to taunt and tease him as he slipped into full-blown panic mode.

His sister, who was with them at the time, ran home to get the babysitter. She returned with the neighbor's who helped get him down. To this day, he can remember everyone on top of the monkey bars that day, and each one of them played a part in his life as time went on. The fear of heights and the reaction of those present played a significant role in shaping his life.

A few years after that, his parents took him and his sister to an amusement park. His parents and the neighbors went on this one particular day. While waiting in line to enter the park, a bird defecated on a man. He carried on for about five minutes. Yelling to his wife that "A bird shit on my head." Others in line chuckling along with everyone Thomas was with. The first ride everyone wanted to do was the Sky Ride. Thomas looked up and did not want to do it. He ended up sitting on a bench with his mother and his friends father as everyone else went on. Those are the only memories he had of that day. His mother stated years later that they brought them to the same park before, that time for the animals. He recalled a few things from that adventure, and he can look back and laugh. He thought he feared an ostrich for the longest time, but now he is more inclined to believe it was an emu. He remembers it came up to the back window on his side and started to peck at the glass. He screamed in terror as it was doing so. His father could not move forward because of other vehicles in line. It seemed like an eternity waiting for him to do so. When he eventually drove off, the emu ran beside the car, neck flailing, and continued to peck at the window as he continued to scream. Years later, while visiting a farm with emu's present, one came up to the fence as he watched and bit him on the hand. To this day, he still doesn't trust them.

Thomas's father eventually found a new job and had to go

away for training. That would leave the kids at home with their mother. One time she dressed up in his old work uniform from a previous job and put a stocking over her head, then came downstairs and scare Thomas and his sister as they clutched onto each other, screaming in terror while their mother laughed. Years later, his father said, "I always wondered why you guys were so glad to see me come home."

The fall of '76 was also the beginning of Thomas's school years. He started out at an elementary school that was only about five blocks from where he lived. His first teacher was an older woman with a raspy voice from years of cigarette smoking. She was very kind and welcoming to everyone. One of Thomas's friends in the neighborhood also started simultaneously, and they walked together every day. She was a blue-eyed, blonde-haired girl. She lived a few houses down with her mother and younger brother. After school, they would come home to watch Bozo the Clown, The Little Rascals, and various other cartoons at the time. His father would be home by that time and usually falling asleep on the couch. There was always a snack at that time, like an upside-down pineapple cake and another cake with peanut butter frosting. He knows where his sweet tooth comes from.

As fall progressed into winter, the sickness started to kick into full gear. Being asthmatic and unable to breathe was a hell that he would not wish upon anyone. His mother would rock him in a chair next to the dehumidifier. Cold and flu season made it even more unbearable. Days spent home on the couch, watching TV with his babysitter or at his grandmother's house. She reminded him of Mama Cass from the Mama and Papas. Hair long and straight, the style of the '70s. TV became his form of entertainment. Cartoons were not on all the time, so he watched many of the older programs that his parents watched. I Love Lucy, M*A*S*H, All in The Family, Sonny and Cher, the list goes on and on. The time spent at his paternal grandparent's house was very special to him. His grandmother being asthmatic herself, understood what it was like for him. He would arrive in the morning, and she would let him watch Captain Kangaroo. Being a asthmatic, she knew how to comfort him, and of course, she would have on hand all of his favorite things, like Rainbow Sherbert ice cream and making various kinds of cookies.

When Thomas did go out in the winter, he could not stay out long. The cold air would tighten up his lungs, making it impossible to stay outside. Sometimes having to wear a mask and being made fun of for doing so. If anyone has ever had difficulty breathing, they would understand the toll it takes on your body. Every muscle in your upper body tightens up, and being so young, he did not understand what was going on and why. Little did he know then of the more challenging times that were to come.

Goodbye

During late spring of this year, Thomas was saying goodbye to an old babysitter. He was homesick at the time, Angie was babysitting him. His parents came home at the same time, which was something that generally had not happened, and his grandmother was with them. She brought Thomas into the kitchen while his parents talked to his baby sitter. His mother said something along the line of "She fainted, and she is having a seizure." Then a short while after that, she had left, and Thomas would not speak to her until many years later. It was a time of extreme sadness for him. It would be a long time before he fully understood and could grasp what had happened.

Her sister ended up taking her place and started to watch Thomas. She watched Thomas for a few years, but Thomas did not bond with her like he did with his previous sitter. She did not watch Thomas for long. She was expecting a baby, and he would not see her again for a few years. Even when he did see her again a few years later, Thomas felt awkward around her. Thomas was in his room putting a model together as he was called down by his mother to see her. He did not stay around long, and he was back in his room, where he felt at peace with himself.

That summer was the release of the movie Star Wars. Thomas and his family watched the film at the local drive-in from the back of a family friend's pickup truck. Thomas enjoyed the movie, and his parents went on to buy many of the action figures thru the years. It was also the summer of rolling blackouts. The power going out for hours at a time. The Son of Sam murders were taking place in another state. Thomas's parents and neighbors were talking about them frequently that summer. Not knowing if the man would come his way. A neighbor that served in Vietnam also came home that summer, and late at night, he would play loud music and occasionally howl. At times he would be seen crawling in the grass. Again an uneasy feeling came across Thomas. That same summer, someone walked into a neighbor's house while drunk and passed out on their couch. A blood trail followed from outside. His parents would take him on bike rides, and the seats for children back then were metal and hinged onto the back. While riding one day, the hinge on the chair he was sitting in loosened up, and Thomas ended up staring at the sky screaming while his head was bouncing off the tire. They laugh now, but back then, it was terrifying. Elvis Presley died that summer, and he can remember everyone being shocked.

Once again, as fall began to set in, he started to become sick again. Cold weather here and there aggravated his asthma. It was on one occasion that stood out amongst the others. His neighbor had come over to check his temperature. As it was so often done during that time, it was done rectally. Thomas kept trying to pull my pajama bottoms down, and his neighbor saying no, you don't need to do that. It was not until years later that this moment would help him understand what had happened.

That Halloween, Thomas picked out the costume he wanted most, and that was of Luke Skywalker, and being disappointed for not being able to show that off. It was so cold that he had to wear a winter jacket. It was also hard enough to snow that night, and Thomas's mask was icing up on the inside with every breathe. It did not stop him and his sister from going with their father.

Thanksgiving was something he always looked forward to. It was a day spent with both sides of the family. One set of grandparents during the day and the other at night. It was at his maternal grandparent's though, that he had the most difficulty. Everyone smoked, and it was a very tiny house that was heated by a fireplace. The clothes Thomas was wearing at the time made him uncomfortable, a turtleneck shirt. The combination of the two made it unbearable for him, often sending him into an asthma attack. His father smoked for many years and smoked in the house for as long as he could remember. Due to the combination of cigarettes, cigars, and wood, the smoke was too much to bear. It was not until years later that his parents started having Thanksgiving at home.

Christmas was more of the same routine. Open gifts at home and then make the rounds all day. He enjoyed being around everyone, but only for a limited time. His parent's made the same decision and decided to stay home a few years later. To him, the holidays were the best of times. It was also around this time that his parents had put their cat to sleep. Thomas didn't understand why they were putting him to sleep and that he was never coming back. He went upstairs and cried. He was the first pet he could remember having despite being a miserable cat. The one memory he had of the cat was while Thomas was on the porch going through baseball cards, and a Black Lab ran onto the porch. The cat chased after the lab, who ran off and never returned.

Another story she spoke of often was how Thomas got into the punch at his Uncles wedding when he was much younger. He strolled back and forth, filling up a cup multiple times and becoming deathly ill because of this. At times he sat and asked himself if it was spiked which he found out that it wasn't.

Good Times

During this winter, Thomas began to use an inhaler. It allowed him to do more, and he could go outside. There were times he used the inhaler and was teased for using it, making him feel awkward. The snow storms that came through were memorable for him. The thoughts that we will be able to get out of the house and get the things they need crossing his mind multiple times. Watching his mother being a nervous wreck. The snowbank in front of his parent's house reached the height of the front porch roof. Thomas wanted to tunnel into it but was told not to, saying it might cave in on him. The same with sliding on this behemoth, being told not to because you may end up being hit by a car. There had not been a winter like that since.

Thomas started to wake up early in the mornings. Usually, about 4 am. It seemed as though every weekend that he woke up, a documentary about Bigfoot was on. With only 13 channels to choose from and most not broadcasting, He watched these, and he would huddle in the middle of the living room, afraid to sit near a window. Thinking if deer and snakes can be in the city, what would stop this. He remembered one scene when homeowners open a door, and the beast was standing there. It terrified him. One day his parents were reading the paper together in the kitchen, and on the front page was a picture with giant footprints. Something he would not forget.

When the programming switched to cartoons, it was a relief for him. He would stay in front of the TV until noon, when the cartoons ended. To think back to the countless bowls of cereal that he ate and ended up spilling milk on the carpet.

Camped out on the living room floor with a blanket and pillow in front of the TV. There were a few times that he got into trouble because the living room smelled of sour milk. But that didn't stop him. He was also a Nestle Quick addict. Glass after glass of chocolate or strawberry milk. He taught himself how to pry the top of the container off using a spoon or knife. He lost track of the countless amount of glasses tipped over. At 1 pm, his favorite show came on, which was a horror flick. They showed classic horror movies. He never missed an episode. After it was over, his mother put him and his sister to work. They would clean the upstairs, and Thomas usually was stuck in the bathroom. One time his mother kept yelling at him for not cleaning behind the toilet. He would go back and do it again. This happened three or four times until he spoke up and said he was doing the best he could to reach behind the tank. She meant the toilet seat.

On Sunday, he would watch movies with his mother. It was usually a horror movie, and it was something they bonded over. That was one of the few things that he could connect with her on.

Thomas was in second grade, and things seemed to be going along smoothly. Being sick was still a significant part of his life. It always seemed like he was ill around a holiday, which led to him not celebrating with kids at school. He was spending most of his time with his grandmother, Occasionally he would have to go to his maternal grandparents, but that was always the last resort. His mother did not want to bring him there, and he never understood why. His grandmother would watch the news, and she would talk to him about what was going on to help him understand the images and chaos being flashed before his eyes. Previews of movies around that time scared the hell out of him. Jaws, The Exorcist, The Omen, to name a few. It was the same for TV shows. Another show they watched frightened Thomas. The sounds and the hand coming out from in front of the tombstone frightened him so.

That summer was spent with the neighborhood kids playing whatever game they could come up with. Thomas was lucky enough to have a pool at this time that his grandparents gave to his family. Of course, he could not swim and held onto the sides for the longest time and just went around the circle. He was very short, and the water was deep. People attempted to show him how to swim, but fear gripped him. Shortly after swimming on one of those days, he and the girl's down the street ended up playing doctor, and Thomas, of course, was the doctor. An innocent child game of exploration. After performing his examination, Thomas and the girl who was disrobed laid down on the bed, and they put a cover over themselves. Thomas again tried pulling down his pants, but the girl had stopped him. His mother ended up walking in on them and abruptly ended that. She found Thomas lying in bed with the other girl, who was not dressed. A tube of toothpaste was lying on the floor next to the bed. His mother was livid. She sent them home and scolded Thomas. His mother kept saying to his father that there was something wrong with him after speaking with him. The next time she brought that up was when he and his friend found his father's porno magazines. And she again walked in on them. Again he was scolded and told how dirty it was, and his friend was sent home. When his father returned, she adamantly said to him that something was wrong with him. It would take many years before he understood why these events would keep coming back to him in his thoughts. It was not until later in life that Thomas would connect these past events that would rattle him to the core and realize that everything he knew was wrong. Thomas was getting in trouble for more things around this time. Small things like using what ever he could find to paint matchbox cars. And it was around this same time that he refused to use the bathroom. Only later in life figuring out why he was doing so. Later that summer, they moved away.

That was also the summer of an energy crisis. His father was talking to his friend one day about how hard it was to get gas. Most of the time was spent at home that summer.

The only other thing that stood out in his mind for that year was the Jonestown Massacre. Jim Jones and the People's Temple. He can still see the images displayed on the screen as a helicopter flew over the scene. The number of people who died was surreal. He could not fathom what happened. Many of those around Thomas at that time also talked about staying away from Moonies. And also being warned to stay away from people in vans for fear of being abducted.

Downward Spiral

Thomas was in second grade at this time. He was not sure of the time of year this next event took place, but it left a mark in his life. While using the bathroom one day, another kid came in while Thomas was there. He was much taller than Thomas was, and he put him against the wall, threatening to beat him up if he did not give him his lunch money. And if Thomas was to say anything to anyone that he would kill him. The effects of that lasted a long time for him. He also found out that his school was closing, and they were being integrated into another school. This made him very nervous, thinking of not being with the kids he was familiar with. Thomas was not looking forward to this. One day while walking home from school, he came across the largest grass snake he had ever seen. At least a couple feet long. It made him paranoid when he walked around, thinking something that large could be anywhere.

Sometime during March, there was a meltdown of a reactor at Five Mile Island Nuclear Facility. It made for an uneasy feeling for Thomas. Everyone talking about radiation and its effects on the environment. He wondered if it would come his way with wind patterns.

During the spring or summer of this year, his uncle was found dead in his apartment. This was the first time he had dealt with death. He didn't understand how someone could just be gone in the blink of an eye. Being so young, he didn't remember much about him. What he did know was that he knew a lot about cars as he was frequently helping his father with his. Later in life, he learned from his grandmother who was told not to look into his death any further because of mafia ties and stolen goods. He was 25 years old.

Summer's around this time frame was spent around Thomas's parent's friends at their house. Lots of swimming, campfires and everyone having fun. Around the 4th of July, they had a tradition that lasted many years. Thomas's neighbor would bring home a road flare, and just after dark, it would be set off; they would run around with sparklers. It would eventually evolve into fireworks as the years progressed. They would order from a magazine, and a large tractor-trailer would pull up out front. They would order a wide assortment of things, and it always began with firecrackers. Thomas's father would sit in the kitchen and read the paper after work. He and his friend would go throw them by the back door of Thomas house. It would and being in between two houses, the echo was immense. Thomas's father would come out of the house yelling, "Cut that shit out." Another time that they set off this multiple rocket launcher. It set off about one hundred whistling rockets, which exploded. After it went off, everyone scattered, knowing the police would come. His mother and neighbor were sitting on the porch as they drove by. And as they did, a large plume of smoke was coming from the driveway. They slowed down, and the police asked if anyone had seen anything, and of course, the reply was no.

Around this time, Thomas also began to learn of colorful family history. On his mother's side, there was Great Aunt who had passed away the previous year. She was a kleptomaniac who had a fetish for ashtray's stuffing them into her purse. When she passed on, his parents gave Thomas and his sister piggie banks filled with change. Thomas later took his to the local department store and dumped all the coins (primarily pennies) on the counter to buy a water-propelled rocket. Then there was Great, Great Uncle, legend has it that he was running booze from Canada in boats during the prohibition era and was chased up a street while being fired upon and hid under a porch.

That summer, he also visited a great uncle and aunt in another state. His only memories of that visit were of his great uncle in an old wooden rocking chair, slowly rocking and silently watching him as he was in the kitchen and again as he moved into a different room. It gave Thomas an uneasy feeling while there. Thomas nor his sister would be left alone during that stay. Years later, he would learn more about him and the horror that took place in that house.

Relatives from his fathers side of the family would visit frequently during the summer. His father's side of the family was more laid back. His great grandfather owned a farm close to town. There was a great Uncle who worked for the a charity. He would stop in and visit while in the area. His Uncle, a stout man, reminded Thomas of John Wayne. His Great Aunt came up to see when she could. They never had children, but they adopted two.

The major news event from this period was that of the Iranian Revolution. In the fall of that year, they took control of the U.S Embassy and taking hostages. Everyone talking about how crazy they were and U.S flags being burned. The Soviet Union had also invaded Afghanistan.

That fall, he began school at the new location. It seemed as though he was always dressed in Garanimal's or corduroy pants. Looking back, Thomas could have started a forest fire had he been outside in those pants. Thomas was very nervous as change is frightening to almost everyone. Going to lunch was also a different experience as the cafeteria was much larger than the previous school. At the beginning of the year, trying to find someone to sit with was a chore. There was a time later that fall that he sat with some people that he was familiar with. He didn't remember the exact question posed to him about girls, but he remembered not having an answer. They laughed, and it was then that he began to feel out of place. He never sat with them again, sitting alone or with other people he could relate to. This started a period in which he didn't want to go to school. The amount of time spent at home during previous years was beginning to show. Thomas couldn't answer question's that were posed to him during class. Some kid's laughing when he did answer. One day Thomas went to school with a pajama top on. His mother had to bring a shirt, and of course, he stood right out as the teacher asked why he was dressed like he was. There was a time Thomas was throwing up in class and being sent home. One particular day his mother had to bring him to school crying because he did not want to be there.

Around the beginning of December, his mother would always talk about starting to put up Christmas decorations. His father never wanted to get into this, and years later, he explained why. It never failed that each year a string of lights would never work. And each year, his father would painstakingly go through the series to find out which bulbs did not work. Some lines caught on fire and some that he just could not figure out. It always left him frustrated, and he would end up going to the reserve center to get away after cursing and swearing. He would always return hours later with a new string of lights. And that is how he earned his nickname Scrooge at Christmas time. Christmas lights were his enemy. He was a short man with an equally short temper that only came out in a tirade of obscenities. This one year before Christmas, he walked in carrying the turkey in one arm. Thomas looked at him and stated. "And there's tiny Tim with his Christmas goose." His father just turned to him and smiled while flipping Thomas the bird. He later explained that he enjoyed Christmas but only Christmas Eve and day. He could care less about the days and weeks leading up to it.

Sickness

The winter of this year was like that of many that had passed. Waking up in the middle of the night, unable to breathe. Thomas's mother or father sitting in the bathroom with him and with a shower in the hottest setting to create a steam room. He would constantly get bronchitis, and it would wear him out. One time, he was given medicine that his parents tried to get him to take, which had a horrible taste. Much worse than that of Robitussin. It burned going down, and they would not let him take a drink of something until a while later. His grandmother was continuously come up with ways to clear the congestion. One that helped was using Vick's in boiling water. Thomas was growing tired of being sick all the time and just wanted to be like everyone else. They brought him in to have allergy tests done, and they told his mother that he was allergic to everything. They talked of removing curtains, carpets, get rid of the pets. It made him feel like he could only live inside an empty box. And it was around this time that they would not let him have chocolate, taking away other favorite things like peanut butter. He didn't feel like a normal kid as others could have whatever they wanted, and these were taken away from him.

One Sunday night during this time frame, there was a large fire at an old manufacturing plant near his house. It lit up the night sky, and you could smell everything burning. It was frightening to him after hearing his mother say something about the fire spreading to other houses. He went to bed that night, wondering if it would come closer to his home.

Around Easter this year, his mother had discussed the

Easter Bunny with him and not hiding eggs. He didn't believe in it at the time, and she said, you're getting too old for that. But she asked him in the form of a question. He felt that if he replied that he still wanted to do it, it was the wrong answer. So he agreed with her and never spoke of it again. But deep down, he still wanted to find those eggs.

Thomas had fallen asleep on the couch one evening and woke to the sounds of his parents talking to their friends. They talked about how they had to fire a babysitter because upon returning home one day, Thomas had a black eye. They were not comfortable with her story, and they let her go.

During May, Mt. St. Helen's erupted, making this a very memorable moment for him. Everyone was glued to their televisions, watching the coverage. There was talk of the amount of ash in the air that would block out the sun affecting the weather and crop growth. Hearing of people and wildlife who passed away in the avalanche of debris from the explosion.

The summer was like that of any other summer. Thomas never wanted summer to end as it was always when he felt his best. Only one moment stands out from that summer for him. It was late evening, and his family was watching TV. Thomas nestled in his usual spot in front of the TV, laying down, as he was the one who had to turn the channels. They had all fallen asleep but quickly woke up to the sound of glass breaking. Someone had thrown a rock through the window. It was later revealed it was meant for a neighbors house. Jacques Cousteau sailed through the Great Lakes that summer, exploring and filming things for a documentary. When his parents mentioned this to him, he spurted out, "The Pink Panther is coming?" Thinking of Inspector Jacques Clouseau of the Pink Panther movies. Of course, they laughed, and he didn't find humor in it.

In April of that year, the United States sent troops to rescue hostages held in Iran. The mission failed. He was always watching TV, and the images of Iranian citizens on the news chanting down with the USA, burning the flag, gave him an uneasy feeling.

That fall started a series of events that would form his life for many years to come. In September of that year, he became very sick and was out of school for weeks, having the worst cough, which led to vomiting. His doctor could not figure out what was going and his mother brought him to the doctor she had worked for at the time to see if he could figure things out. There was one night he was lying on the couch watching America Werewolf in London. His parents were visibly frustrated, telling him to take a drink of water to try and stop the cough. The couch would lead to Thomas vomiting. Nothing was working. A few days later, his mother brought him to the hospital, and he was admitted. He spent another two weeks in the hospital hooked up to IVs, He started to get better, and they removed the IVs for about a day, and then he began to slip backward. That night they had to put the IVs back in and didn't want them to. Breaking down in tears. He was tired of everyone poking into his arms and feeling weak. That next day his family priest came in, but he could he was in and out of sleep due to exhaustion. A new doctor had come to town, and she was brought in to figure out what was going on. She did a throat culture, something he would never forget. The results came back that he had a Whooping cough. By the time he was out of the hospital, it had been about a month. He was unable to do school work during this time and had mounds of paperwork to catch up on. His parents tried to help him catch up with this, but he did not understand it. Upon going back to school, he was so far behind everyone. At this time, they were learning multiplication. He was doing 1x1, and everyone else was at 4's and 5's. It was at this point that he said to his parents that he did not understand it. But to him, it fell on deaf ears.

That September, the news was on Tylenol's killing and warning everyone not to take it. It was another scary moment for him, thinking of all the times he had to take it with fevers running high.

In December of that year, John Lennon was killed. Thomas's mother was making jawbreakers and chocolates for the holidays like she always did at that time of the year. She grew up a fan of the Beatles and often spoke of watching them on TV. That evening they went to his great aunt's house to decorate. Everyone decorated, but he was just not in the mood. She had an old piano that she used to play and sing on holidays. Every kid that went in the house attempted to play that piano, She played that night, and it was moments like this that he will never forget.

Falling Into Despair

The winter of this year was like that of any other. There were still times that he was sick, and other times he made himself sick with worry. He was unable to grasp all of the information that the teachers were throwing at him. Time out of school was spent sparingly with his grandmother. His grandfather was still battling his illness which he found out was testicular cancer. The rest of his time was spent with aunts and uncles and a neighbor. His uncle spent one weekend with him, and they formed a bond that he will forever remember. His parents had traveled to another state, and of course, he was sick, and they spent the weekend watching sci-fi movies and talked about a wide range of topics. His uncle spoke about Bigfoot, UFOs and telling him stories of times he went hiking and camping. He enjoyed that weekend. His aunt watched him on a couple of occasions, and one time stood out amongst the others, and that was when they played hide and seek. She hid in the closet, but when it was time for her to come out, a Lincoln Log jammed the door. She started to panic, of course, which led Thomas and his sister into tears. They fondly looked back at that moment and laughed.

That spring was his family's first trip to South. They drove there with his parent's friends. At a rest stop it became embedded in his mind that he could not eat corn dogs because it just did not agree with him, and it was not until he was an adult that he had another. The first hotel they stayed at was a short stay. Once entering the elevator, it smelled of urine. And upon entering the room, it did not improve as the beds were full of sand. They spent the night, but upon waking the following day, a walk on the balcony to see a green pool and lounge chairs floating in it ended that stay. Can't always go by a brochure. They stopped at a spot for pizza, which he will never forget, only because of the hearse out front. They did have a great time, though he would not go on any rides at the amusement park again. He was afraid of going into the ocean at first because of Jaw's movie, but that did not stop him. By the end of that vacation, he did not want to go back to school.

March of that year, there was an attempt to assassinate President Ronald Reagan. It was all over the networks watching and replayed many times over the following weeks. It was a moment he will never forget.

That summer was like that of any other. Having a summer birthday and a pool was always a delight. Around this time, he began to wonder why his maternal grandparents were never around for his birthday. Every year they would drop off a gift but not stay. It was the first time he noticed a pattern. His grandfather would always go out in the yard and look in the trash first before coming in. It only happened by chance that he noticed this. Knowing now that he was born in the era of the depression and looked for anything he could use. His grandfather was eccentric. He had his ways, and there was no stopping it. During holidays he would be drinking Pabst Blue Ribbon with his cigar and talk about his days in the military. Saying I sailed the seven seas, don't believe me ask my boys, with one eye squinting. He was a hoarder and reused many items. Straightening nails and reusing many items was a common thing for him.

His Grandfather drank often, and it was then that he became belligerent. Thomas remembers walking behind him as he went down to the basement with a beer in hand, tripping and falling ass over tea kettle to the bottom. He did not spill a bit of that beer. Thomas's grandparents slept in the basement. There was also a bar and pool table. A vintage radio sat in the corner with a giant dial that Thomas often looked at and played with. Imagining it was the 1940's and broadcasts of the war coming across. All the guys would be down there during the holidays playing pool. By the end of the night, his grandfather would be saying, "You don't understand." As he reminisced about his days during the war. One night as Thomas's family was heading home, his father yelled back at him. "Go back to your bomb shelter."

That fall, he started the 5th grade, and he continued to fail at school. At one point, he was not doing his homework. He just didn't understand it, and nobody could help him at that point. After he received the first report card, he tried to tell his parents that he didn't understand anything, and their reply was if your sister could do it, then so could he. But it didn't come across that way to him. He didn't feel wise at all, and when he told them the way he felt, it was met with the replies of "Don't Be Ridiculous" and "That's not true." Like his feelings were not valid. To him, it felt like they didn't care what he thought and that he should have better marks than he had. He started to shut down. Thomas's grades were always compared to others and he struggled to get through each day. Shortly after that incident, his teacher had called his father into school because he was not receiving his homework. Some stuff was left in his locker, and the rest he does not remember where it was. His father put him up against the wall by his neck and said if he didn't straighten his act out there would be trouble. From that point on, he was frightened of him. Looking back, he started to build resentment towards others because the work was so easy for her.

Sometime in October of this year, while Thomas was home again from school, President Anwar Sadat of Egypt was assassinated during a military parade. His grandmother was watching the news at the time. He also remembers images of the Iraq-Iran war. She again tried to explain the pictures of what was happening and the chaos of the world. Thomas talked to a friend later in life, and she stated that he always seemed to be thinking big thoughts. Reflecting on these moments, it made sense to try to process these moments as seen on TV while being homesick and kids his age were off doing what all kids do.

He started to spend more time in his room. His fascination began with military aircraft, and he began to study military history not only of the U.S but throughout the world. He also started building military models and trying to make them look as authentic as possible. He was not interested in learning what was taught at school except when it came to history. And it was around this time that he had a crush on Daisy Duke of the Dukes of Hazzard. He had cut out a picture from a magazine and had it in his room. Of course, everyone teased him in the house, shutting him down more.

Spiral Continues

In the winter of this year, Thomas's parents had bought an Intellivision game system, and when he was home, he played as much as he could. His father also played with him at various times, but it was not often because he was so busy working and on some weekends with the military. He enjoyed these moments because they never really had been able to spend time together.

In March of this year, they went back to the south, and by this time, their friends had a condominium, and they stayed in a hotel. Thomas was excited because they would be near an air base with the F-14 Tomcat aircraft, and he was anxiously waiting to see flying overhead. When they did, he was looking to see what type it was, whether cargo or fighter. They did go fishing a few times on a pond close by to the condo, but he was very nervous after being told to watch out for alligators. Upon returning home and starting back at school, the Falkland Island's war had begun as the British Navy had sailed towards after Argentina had invaded the British Isles. Thomas watched as much as he could to see the operations take place. Especially that of the Hawker Harrier doing a vertical take-off which amazed him.

Later that spring, his friend's mother talked about getting him involved in playing Baseball. She thought it would be good for him, but his mother kept saying he could not play because of asthma. He didn't have an opinion on this as she made that decision for him. It was then that he began to believe he couldn't do it and had limited capabilities.

That summer, Thomas and and his friend built a platform in the upper part of his friends garage. They used any kind of wood they could find while using his father's tools. After Thomas's father was done work that day and told him what they did, he was not very happy because they used some of the wood he wanted for another project. And to top it off, he found his skill saw with the cord partially cut and wrapped around the blade. By the end of summer, Thomas had come down with the chickenpox, which he could not stand. School had just started, and again he could not go.

Sixth Grade was not any easier for Thomas as his struggles continued. He just wanted to fit in at school but always felt out of place. He was out of school when they were given the assignment to do a commercial that was to be recorded. When he returned, everyone had already picked what they were doing and who they would work with. He did complete it on his own, but he could have cared less about doing that project. His parents were also called to school because he would not take a shower after gym. Many others in his class had started puberty at this time, and he hadn't, again being teased. He was unable to explain to his parents why he wouldn't shower. He could not find the words.

Thomas's father had fallen down the stairs that fall, tripping over a vacuum that Thomas's mother had left at the top of the stairs. His little toe was almost severed off. It was a scary moment for Thomas, having never seen his father in that kind of situation and viewing him as invincible. It was towards December that an incident took place that he looked back at and laughed. Thomas and his sister were the last ones at the table. She said something to him that ticked him off, and he dumped her glass of milk on her plate. She yelled, "Daddy," and he knew he was in trouble. He got up quickly as his father hobbled out to the kitchen in his sock feet. Thomas moved as fast as he could as his father went to swat at him, but his father's foot was on a throw rug, and the momentum kept him going as he ended up crumpled in a ball at the door. He ran upstairs and locked the door. His mother came up shortly after and told him not to come downstairs as his father was angry but was in too much pain to move. He stayed in there for the night, and his sister ended up doing dishes.

Every December was the start of holiday programming, which he always enjoyed watching with his mother. They would talk about what was coming on and which night it would be on. One show that she liked would be on, and he went out to the kitchen to let her know. He said, "The show you like is going to be on with the guy you like, Red Skeleton." She laughed and said, "Red Skelton." Though to Thomas, it was not funny, and he ran off upset. At the time, they didn't know of the number of times he had been laughed at for not knowing something.

An Upward Trend

The winter of this year was a continuation of previous winters. Thomas was sick on and off due to bronchitis and others due to worry and making himself sick. Thomas had been collecting stamps at this point and was learning history around the world. He brought an album from his collection he had to school for show and tell. As Thomas was was presenting, a pill dropped on the floor; by this time, Thomas had grown tired of the countless medications being given to him. This was one that he hid, and the teacher noticed it and asked what that was. He spurted out that it was the cat's pill. His parents were called in about that, and they watched him take that medication daily.

Around April of this year, the news was still on happenings in the Middle East. By now, Thomas was watching the news daily. This one day, it was of the U.S Embassy bombing in Beirut, Lebanon. A truck outside exploded. Months later, there was another bombing. One that was outside U.S Marine barracks. Everyone feared they were going to end up in a war.

Come May, his parents went to school to discuss if Thomas would move on to 7th Grade. The teachers wanted him to be held back, but his parents thought it was best if he moved on with everyone else—Thomas was to be advanced to Junior High. Years later, he had talked to his father about it and wondered what it might have been like had he been held back. His father stated they thought he should move on with friends, while Thomas often thought of what it would have been like had he been held back. They understood each other after they talked.

That summer was spent with his grandparent's camping. Something they had done many previous summers, and he always looked forward to. His grandparents owned a large camper and would go to the local campgrounds. Thomas and his sister would go with them for a week at a time. He would always sleep on the top bunk. He would wake up to the smell of bacon that his grandmother was cooking on the propane stove. She would always have the small boxes of cereal that they could choose from. After breakfast, Thomas would help his grandfather with the wood for fires at night. Thomas and his grandmother would always be on the lookout for ducks and feed them bread. It was the simple things he enjoyed the most.

While his father was away at training this year, his mother watched Friday the 13th Part II one night. At the time, it scared him to death as Jason jumped through the window bringing him back to the moments of watching Bigfoot documentaries at 4 am while sitting in the middle of the living room. That night he had to sleep on his sister's floor because he was so freaked out because of that movie.

That Fall, he started at the new school with plenty of fresh faces and unfamiliar grounds. There was one kid that grabbed a handful of dead flies and stuffed them in his mouth, and then proceeded to chase someone. There was one kid in gym class who could not swim and held the walls of the large pool. Bringing back memories of Thomas as a child doing the same and feeling sorry for him because others laughed as he did so. There was another kid he met that relocated from the south, and he befriended Thomas. People would occasionally want to start fights with him, and he always held his ground. He didn't want to be put into that position, but circumstances always warranted him to do so. He would end up playing a more significant role in Thomas's life at a later time. Again things in the class were hard for him to grasp. The only class he excelled in was History;

Math was always a weak spot for him. Lunchtime was not any easier. He knew and sat with people there, but the conversations did not get any easier. Madonna was big around that time, and a discussion came up at the table about her. When his opinion was asked, he didn't know how to respond and turned red. And, of course, everyone laughed, and Thomas did his best to avoid those conversations. And it was just another reason why he didn't want to go to school.

The Invasion of Grenada took place in October of that year, and he was more interested in those events than anything else.

School Issues

By the beginning of this year, Thomas was starting to find ways not to go to school. Besides the occasional bout with bronchitis, there were times that his stomach was off. Throwing up at times and unable to keep things down. At some point during this school year, he did have a crush on one girl in class. She was blonde and had a southern accent. Her name would be etched in his mind for years to come. He eventually carved her name into some wood in his room like an end table, a shelf, or other things. Not one of the most innovative things to do by any means his mother found these things; she was livid, which is understandable. But what happened next was a pattern that would repeat itself many times over the years. She would call all of her sisters and his grandparents and tell them what she found. Of course, he was mortified, but what happened days later put the icing on the cake. Word had gotten back to school through a cousin, and people were relentless in teasing him about it. Saying there she is as he walked down the hall or comes into class. As time went on, the same thing was happening at home. His parents and his sister would say her name and tease him about it laughing. To him, it was not funny at all as he could not escape it. Had they known what was happening at school, they would not find humor in it. But by this time, he was already under the impression that nobody understood him nor cared. He lacked self-esteem and confidence and built the walls up to remain around him for many years to come. From that moment on and for many years, he would come home from school, go to his room, listen to music, and work on a model. That was his escape from all the chaos. He just went through the motions at school, trying to do homework and knowing the answers were wrong. It didn't matter to him at all. By the end of the school year, he was destined to go to summer school.

That summer was spent mainly in school. He was told he had to be in bed at a particular time and couldn't do much of anything else. Thomas ended up taking 3 classes, and he did pass them but just by a narrow margin. He benefited from the smaller class size, and he was able to grasp some of the concepts. Looking back at these times, he was always looking out the window daydreaming. Thomas felt he had the attention span of a circus monkey.

In English class, he had to write a poem and recite it in class which Thomas dreaded and avoided doing at all costs. He eventually did the project, which he did receive a bad grade, but the whole process to get that done took a toll on him.

That summer, he watched a concert by a music group that would stay with me to this very day. It was U2 Live at Red Rocks. The energy and stage presence they brought forth was intoxicating to him. He watched that many times over that summer and was excited when he found out that they would release a new LP that fall.

As the holidays approached, there was less desire to be around his family. Everyone was coming to his house, and he would stay downstairs just long enough to be seen. Thoughts of his mother telling everyone the things he was doing or going through echoed in his mind. Everyone would talk over one another, which would lead to him having a headache and not knowing what to say to anyone. He would head back to his room and lay down on the bed and turn some music on or just drift off to sleep. It would remain this way for many years to come.

Things Are Looking Up

The winter of this year continued like that of many past. Thomas would be sick at times from bronchitis and from times of worry. He worried about not having homework complete and what would be said in class. There was a day when Thomas had bronchitis, and his father was so tired of hearing him cough that he gave him NyQuil at 7 am. It did not sit well, and he ended up vomiting in the kitchen sink. He had heard this, and when he came downstairs, he immediately gave him another dose. He was in a coma until 4 pm that day.

There were days when Thomas didn't go to class because of unfinished homework or to gym class. Gym class was never a favorite for him. He didn't want to play Dodge ball or swim because of acne. He didn't want to attempt to ski for fear of falling and being laughed at. He didn't have a hat to go skiing a day, and the teacher tried to provide one for him, which he refused. He spoke up and said he was not wearing the hat they dug out of a box because he didn't know whose head it was on or washed. Detention started to become a regular activity for him after school. He would go to the nurse's office to escape these times with an upset stomach. Sometimes he would go home and other times lay there for the longest time. The nurse at this time was also the same nurse that was in his elementary school. She knew him well and knew when he was faking it and when it was real. She retired shortly afterward this period, and his connection with her would play a more significant role in the future with someone he would be in a relationship with. This woman would help shed light on the dark days of his past.

This year was also the summer of knee-high tube socks,

shorts with a white stripe down each side. This is one style he prayed that will never come back into fashion. Thomas's neighbor had a foreign exchange student from Germany who came to stay for the following school year. He had a unique style, and they learned about his life in Germany and how it differed from theirs. It was then that Thomas became interested in other cultures. They could not get him to be very sociable as all he wanted to do was watch MTV at the time. When they did get him away from the TV, it was very entertaining. Thomas's sister taught them a new game using a shot glass and quarters. They played this on his parent's antique kitchen table, and bouncing the quarters off the table left many marks on it, which their mother was not very pleased with. They were not drinking alcohol, but it was fun. Live-Aid was the big event of the summer, and they were glued to every minute of it. Simultaneous Concerts being broadcast around the world on MTV.

That Fall, he entered the 9th grade, and he started in the regent's portion of it. The previous year he thought that if he could do this and put the effort to feel some kind of acceptance from his parents. It didn't last long, and he was put back into the non-regents classes. Thomas looked at it as a failure and continued to beat himself up over this.

As Winter approached, Asthma was no longer an issue with him. His father had quit smoking in the house, and he was not having bouts of bronchitis that he had in the past. His confidence was still at an all-time low. He did hang out with friends from the neighborhood but not much more outside of that. He could stay out longer in the winter and could do what everyone else was doing, like plugging cars with snowballs, hooking the UPS truck. Thomas made up for all the years of not being able to go outside.

Building Confidence

This year began with the Space Shuttle Challenger exploding in the air after taking off. He could imagine the fear in the minds of the astronauts as this event unfolded. These images were replayed over and over for many days following this. He often pictured himself afterward being in a plain and having a scenario like that happen. It did make him nervous about flying.

In April, there was an explosion of a nuclear reactor in Chernobyl, Soviet Union. This once again stoked fears of radiation poisoning as radiation spewed into the air and landed in several surrounding countries. It was not contained till May, and people were evacuated, making the area inhabitable.

By May of this year, it was the beginning of his love for baseball. One day at his maternal grandmother's, he watched a game with his uncle. The Cincinnati Reds were on, and Tom Browning was pitching. His uncle taught him about the game, and as he watched in amazement as Browning would throw the heat and drop Lord Charlie in on a batter. The batter wanted to swing, but his knees became weak and he was struck out.

By Summer Thomas and his friends were having their pickup games in the neighborhood. His neighbor, who played softball at this point, gave him lots of tips about pitching. Thomas ate up every bit of information he threw at him. Arm angles, windup, and pitching grips. They played every day from morning until dusk, occasionally stopping to jump in the pool to cool off only to start back up. And in the evenings, the games would come on, and they would be glued to the TV. The post-game would come on, and he would learn more about handling the bat. He found out that when you see the ball, it is as large as a beach ball and just floats into the plate. And when you in a slump, you don't even see it leave the pitcher's hand. This was one of the few times he remembers his father trying to connect with him. After playing ball all day and sitting down to dinner, he would ask him questions about baseball and how it was going. And when Thomas was watching the Reds, he would ask how they were doing. Around this time, Thomas's father told him he used to love baseball as a kid and was an Indians fan. Over the years, they would continue to talk baseball on occasion, and these are moments he looked back on fondly.

That summer, Thomas went camping in the woods with 2 of his Uncles and friends. One of Thomas's friends was adamant that he would not be able to complete this only because he was a football player and conditioned for it, and Thomas did not play any sport at that time. And that Thomas was not going to make it in the military. Thomas had no problem with the ten-mile hike in, and they set up camp near a waterfall. They had no radio and no outside contact with the rest of the world, and his Uncle would tell stories about UFO abductions and all kinds of wilderness stories. They spent about 4 days at the spot and then began the journey out. They then went about halfway and camped out for the night. The waterfalls had drowned out any activity that was happening at first sight. This site turned out to be one of the longest nights of Thomas's life. They were near a lake, but there was no wildlife activity at all. The birds were quiet, and they all had a sense of being watched. They were all tired and ready to head home the next day. One of his Uncles had started a fire that night while the rest of them laid down to get ready for the last day's hike. As it began to get dark, there was the sound of large branches breaking. His Uncle became nervous and decided he was going into his tent. That was a night that never seemed to end. At one point, something ran through the camp, and they could feel the ground shake. They could see the moonlight through the tent flaps, and something went past, blocking the light. It could have been a bear, Deer, and of course, they all joked, saying it was Bigfoot. His friend, who was in his tent, woke up once yelling, "They are coming after me," as he sat up. Needless to say, they wasted no time in leaving the area and getting back to their rendezvous point. His friend on the way out whined and complained the whole time as he carried the pots and pans, which kept hitting the back of his legs. Thomas's Uncle threw a stick at him at one point, telling him to shut up. Thomas ended up carrying them the rest of the way. Afterward, his Uncle commented about how well he did and how he will never go with his friend again. There was talk about doing that again, and he was looking forward to it, but as fate would have it, they never returned.

Later that summer, something happened that was to be engraved in Thomas's mind to this day. While sitting on the porch with music playing, Thomas caught something out of the corner of his eye. Thomas jumped up and ran off the porch to see an object with a blueish glow around the center. With red strobe lights on top and bottom. It made no noise whatsoever. Thomas was studying military aircraft for a couple of years at the point, and he knew what was out there. This was something he had never seen before or since. He ran to the yard in disbelief of what he had just witnessed and watched until it disappeared. Soon after that, Thomas had a family reunion, and he and his Uncle discussed it, and his Uncle had seen the same thing. It left him with an eery feeling. Thomas and his Uncle became closer that fall as he helped him with his homework. He was brilliant and showed him easier ways to answer questions. He was a History teacher at another school. Thomas's grades began to improve, and so did his confidence. He can remember at one point becoming jealous because of his friends who would go hang out with his Uncle when he couldn't.

Later that fall, it felt like Thomas had lost his best friend as he ended up in a psychiatric ward. He was not going to work, and when they found him, he was trying to dig into his ears with a pencil to get the transmitters out that the aliens had put in. Thomas returned to work, and it was challenging to have conversations with him. And soon after, his uncle was placed on dialysis with kidney disease that would run rampant in his family. Thomas's friends asked how he was doing at times, and he explained the best that he could. But he never mentioned to them that they both saw the same object in the night sky for fear of being laughed at.

Finding His Way

This year was the beginning of a turning point for Thomas. In April, U2 released The Joshua Tree, which shot them into stardom. His friend played guitar, and it was soon after they started playing around musically. He had an electronic drum kit, and they would play along to the music. Thomas was not good on the drums, but he was learned to play some bass guitar. Another friend came along, and they spent some time jamming in his father's garage. Thomas played the bass, first learning Uncomfortably Numb by Pink Floyd. He couldn't read the music, but if he listened, he could pick up the chords. And eventually, he tried his hands on the guitar, which he loved and often borrowed from his friend, and practiced some songs. Thomas always wanted to get a guitar, but it never ended up happening.

His friend decided Thomas needed a makeover, and it was then that his appearance changed. It all started with a haircut, spiked hair at that. It was not long after that the clothes that Thomas wore altered also. His confidence was growing though he was still timid. Thomas had his sister picking out the clothes he was to wear and what clothes to buy. At one point, he began to bleach his jeans.

That summer was spent playing more baseball and playing against kids from other neighborhoods. A girl in the area Thomas hung around them all the time because her brother played ball on his team. She annoyed the hell out of him at times, but he still liked her. He would have dated her, but she was a few years younger than he was, and the thought of being teased more by my friends prevented him from doing so. There was no doubt that the feelings were mutual, but he did not want to go there. They would spend the summers swimming, playing Marco Polo, chase tag, and many other games. Innocent games that he enjoyed because of not being able to play them as much as a child. Her parents ended up taking him to a Cincinnati Reds ballgame that summer. Mario Soto pitched a shut-out against the Montreal Expos. Eric Davis hit a home run. A night he will never forget.

That fall, he had saved up enough money and went to his first concert, U2, of course. His father drove Thomas and his friend to the show, waited for them in the car, and read his book. They had floor tickets and about 10 rows back from the stage. His father started listening to the music Thomas listened to and liked some of it. This was just one example of the kind of things he would do for his kids.

During this time, while at lunch with all of the guys hanging around at the table, a change occurred. There were many previous times while at lunch the subject of girls would come up and of course he became embarrassed. The guy would laugh and make comments about his ears turning red because of embarrassment. And they would call him "Ears." But when he was given the nickname Radar, the guys took it to the next level and dubbed him "Radar the Red-Eared Retard." After a few times of this happening, he finally stood up for himself and challenged a guy to a fight. He was much bigger than Thomas was, a country boy who worked on his family farm, and Thomas knew he did not stand a chance against him.

Many tried to talk Thomas out of this fight, including his friend. His friend would play a much more significant role in Thomas's life in later years. That afternoon they were to fight, and many people tried to talk him out of it, but he knew he did not have a choice. And as it played out, his instincts were correct. He knocked Thomas out and woke up in a daze in the back of his friends car. Upon arriving home, he cleaned himself up before his parents came home. When his mother caught the first sight of him, her first reaction was to call the school. Thomas did not want that, and thankfully his father talked her out of it. Thomas didn't go to school for a few days. When he did return, those words were never uttered again. They became good friends shortly after that. Respect had been earned.

Thomas's appearance around this time also changed, and people were starting to take notice. He always had music playing in his locker between classes, and he always had some kind of candy, gum of some sort on hand. Some people were charged, and some were not. Some females, of course, he would give it to them for free. He was still timid, but he was beginning to open up.

Awkward Moments

Thomas's attendance at school was increasing throughout the winter, and he wanted to be in school as much as possible. He did not want to be home and made every attempt to be there. Around this time, there was a string of girls who had come into his life. He was still uncomfortable at times talking to people. One he had started to date. She was beautiful, with brown hair and brown eyes. It did not last long as it ended up she slept with someone else at a party, which devastated him. At the time, he felt betrayed. Someone else came along shortly after that and she was in the class behind him. She wanted to walk home with him one day, and they talked the whole way. She was also beautiful, and Thomas could not figure out why she wanted to spend time with him. He almost had a date with her as they talked about watching a movie. The problem was he did not have a license at the time and, of course, not relating to girls he didn't know how to recover. It was a regret that he carried with him for a long time.

That summer was unlike that of any other. This was the summer that he started listening to Van Halen 5150. Summer nights. Thomas's friend at the time and someone he has not spoken to spent that summer fishing along the lake in many years. His friend would get beer from his father's stash or Thomas's father's and head to his great uncle's camp along the lake. Start a fire on the rocks along the shore, crack a beer, and cast out a line.

It was around this time that he began to have a reoccurring dream. It was that of driving along a stretch of highway that had had water on both sides. It was peaceful, and he would cross a bridge that had a high peak at one point in the dream. A few years later, this would come into play in his life in a profound way.

That Fall, he started his Senior year. Thomas was ready for what the future held at that point. He was nervous but wanted to get away from the suburban life that he had grown to know. Thomas had thought of going to college. He dreamed of traveling to distant lands and seeing all that he could see.

Having Fun

The winter of this year was spent prepping for a small college he was to attend. Nervousness played a part in his everyday life. Not knowing what to expect and where he was heading in life. He did not pick a job before going into the service. He was not quite sure what he wanted to do. Most of his friends had chosen what career path they wanted to follow. Watching the events unfold during the invasion of Panama didn't help, but he knew that was a decision he wanted to follow through on. Schoolwork was becoming easier for him, and one day during this time, he had one class in the morning, and the rest of the day was study halls. He would sign out on that day at 9:30 am and head home to do things to help out his father. Looking back, he could see that he was a people pleaser. It was the only way he could receive any recognition and gratification. He would help anyone he could and continues to do so until this day.

As spring approached, his friends talked about the Senior Dinner Dance. He did not go to prom in the 11th grade but decided to go to this. He managed to get along with everyone. He treated everyone the same regardless of their situation and continues to do so. His friend went with a popular girl, and Thomas went with one of her friends. He was nervous, but he fought through it and ended up having a great time. They ended up going into Canada for dinner. Of course, everyone was ordering different mixed drinks and beer; Thomas was drinking coffee around this time, and he decided to go with an Irish Coffee. The amount of whiskey they put in it was robust, but it was loaded with flavor. They had a great time at the dance, though he didn't dance to any fast songs, he did with slow songs. His friend was the same way. The night ended on a happy note as they dropped Thomas's date off first. He walked her to the back door, and that was the moment of his first kiss. He was nervous, as was she. Their friends honked the car horn and flashed the lights as they kissed. They laughed, and of course, their friends joked with Thomas as he got back into the car. He felt on top of the world at that moment. He knew, though, that they would go their separate ways, and he eventually lost contact with her.

That June, upon receiving his last report card, he discovered he was short one credit and was told he could not graduate without it. But looking a little deeper, he noticed he did not receive credit for a class he had taken. He raced around the school and finally had it all together. He ended up just getting through school with a 75-grade average. He did not want his parents to throw him a party, but they did anyway. He felt awkward and didn't want his friends there. It was agreed that he only had to stay there for a short period, only because he wanted to go to other parties.

As the summer went on, he started to say goodbye to the people he knew. Everyone went their separate ways, not knowing if they would see each other again. At the time, Thomas was working as a janitor at his church. His friend's brother ended up getting him a job at a Pizzeria as a cook. The day he told him about it, Thomas was sitting in front of the TV watching events unfold at Tiananmen Square in China. As one man stood in front of a tank. The job paid more money, and he decided why not. He had worked with various people through the years, usually with a neighbor building things and working on his camp or mowing lawns for people. This job opened the door to more pay and meeting different people.

His time at the pizzeria was memorable for him. There was a guy who was ex-Navy and also a cook. A very nervous fellow who was always on edge. While cooking, and when he thought nobody was looking, he would stuff his mouth with sausage or pepperoni. This always gave Thomas a chuckle. He found out years later that he was found dead outside of his house next to his vehicle. He slipped on the icy stairs striking his head. Thomas managed to get along with everyone while he worked there. These were carefree days for him while he waited to enter the service. One moment he never forgot was a day that kids on skateboards refused to leave the parking lot, creating a hazard for drivers and putting themselves in danger. They asked them politely to go, and they mouthed off to the workers. They eventually made their way into the restaurant and proceeded to order, and the other cook and Thomas made sure they were served correctly. They took the dough out, dropped it on the floor, left debris on it, and placed it back in the pan. They each took a milk drink and spit on it multiple times and then put their pizza together. They had a good laugh about it afterward, watching them devour the pizza and not knowing what had been done.

The rest of that fall and into the onset of winter was spent working and occasionally attending parties with people at work. Thomas was still timid, but he was able to carry on a conversation with everyone. There were three girls that he had worked with who he found very attractive. At the time, Thomas was still a virgin, and they knew it. And Thomas can't be sure on one of them, but two of them tried to get with him, which he did not pursue. One of them, a thin bubbly brunette, whispered in his ear during a party one night that she wanted him. Thomas wanted to, but he held on to his belief in waiting, which nobody knew about him. And getting ready to leave for the college and going about his plans that he wanted to see come to fruition. He acted like he didn't hear her. He ended up leaving that night, and nothing happened.

The second girl Thomas and his friend partied with one night led to some hot and heavy kissing but nothing more. She had been around the block and had a child at this point. His friend at the time, who had been with her previously, told him beforehand that it was like sliding in between two pieces of roast beef. The third, he ended up driving home, and she invited me up to her apartment. She was a platinum blonde beauty who he knew from school and was very attracted to. Again he could sense where things were going, and again he did not strike at the opportunity laid before him. He had to get his father's vehicle back to him and again held to his beliefs.

The company Christmas party was held a few houses down from his grandmother's house, and it was a blast. Everyone had a great time, and he remembered at one point walking out onto the porch to urinate because the bathroom was unavailable the majority of the time. One time while he was outside, his grandmother walked by with her dog. She did not recognize him at all. Though she mentioned days later about the party and the incident, she didn't know it was him.

As it turned into the new year and as the time grew closer for him to leave, the nervousness about the next part of his life was starting to take hold. He believed at the time that he would go to school, have a couple of kids, a house, and enjoy life. The day he left, it was snowing heavily, and he started to think he would be snowed in. Part of him would not have minded staying another day, but he was anxious to get moving forward. His parents drove him to the bus station, and they said their goodbyes. As he got onto the bus and found a seat, he stared out the window listening to music and wondering what he was getting into? Did he make the right choice? Life was about to become much more interesting.

CHAPTER 2

A New Journey

Thomas arrived at his hotel that evening not sure what to expect from the coming days. That night he was restless, anticipating the a fresh start in a new location. After a quick breakfast, he started to walk to find his way around. He made his way to the airport and the thought of that flight made Thomas very nervous as he recalled the various plane crash reports he had watched on the news growing up. The flight was cancled and he ended up spending the night in the airport. It was at this time that he met someone that was going to the same school as he was. The following morning their flight departed and as the flight taxied down the runway, Thomas clutched the handles of his seat and began to speak louder as the flight ascended into the clouds. His nerves calmed as the flight went on, only to peak again during periods of turbulence and upon landing. The weather again forced them to spend that night in the airport and delaying their arrival. They would end up staying there for a day.

Coming Into His Own

Thomas headed back to college after the holidays. He arrived at temperatures in the 80's but while up north, he became sick and was still feeling the effects of that. Over the next few weeks, Thomas began to sleep more and more. This lasted for a few weeks, and at the time, Thomas thought nothing of it. Years later, he would realize it was a pattern. His friends asked him what was wrong and why he was sleeping so much, but he brushed it off. At this time, his friends ended up pulling a prank that would last for many months. When Thomas woke up after sleeping the day away, he could smell lotion. He had lotion on his hands and face with some covering his pillow. He laughingly confronted his roommate and friends with whom they shared a bathroom and denied knowing or saying who did what. It became an all-out war. The toilet seat was covered with saran wrap. Throwing powder in each other's faces when it was least expected. Two pranks put the game over the top. One by Thomas and the other was by his friend. In the south, they kept open boxes of food in the mini-fridge they had in their rooms. One day Thomas opened his fridge to grab a drink, but the refrigerator smelled of rotten fish. He could not understand where this was coming from as there was not much inside. It then occurred to him to look at the open box of Corn Flakes, and upon doing so, the odor was more pungent. Back in the 1970's they would put toys in the cereal boxes, which Thomas and his sister would argue over. As he emptied the box into a bowl, a used condom tumbled out. Thomas was disgusted but also laughing as he knew he had to top that. It took a few days, and Thomas figured out what he was going to do.

WITHOUT A VOICE

Since they shared a bathroom, Thomas went in and grabbed his friends bottle of shampoo. He proceeded to urinate in the half-empty bottle and stirred it with a broken plastic hanger, placing the toxic combination back in its original place. Thomas then waited and kept an eye on the bottle until it was thrown out. Thomas then asked him what kind of shampoo he used because his hair had a nice sheen. As his friend was telling him, Thomas laughed and told him, "I pissed in your shampoo bitch." and "You have been walking around smelling like a nursing home for weeks." his friend chased after Thomas, but Thomas got away in time. A truce was called at that point.

Around this time, Thomas was coming into his own. The college gave him a message to call his parents because they had not heard from him. He had not realized it had been weeks since he had talked to them, almost a month. He spoke with his father and explained that he had been busy with friends and his father only asked in return that he check in once in a while.

On January 17th, operations began in the Middle East. They watched on TV thinking of their friends who were over there and hoping they were safe. Scud missiles being launched in every direction. The day the ground invasion started, they learned that troops went into Iraq and Armed Forces Radio played The Clash Song Rock the Casbah. Fitting for what was taking place.

As the war began to wind down, people that had gone began to return later that summer. One friend from highschool came back a mess. For the first few months back, he would get up in the middle of the night and crawl into his locker. He would spend the rest of the night in there with a flashlight. The frequent air raid sirens that activated during the war affected him in so many ways. It took a long time for him to overcome that.

At dropped out of college and began to work, Thomas was coming into his own. He had built so much confidence within himself, and it showed. College was the first time in his life where he had come across so many different cultures. But he was easy to get along with, and others noticed. Everyone on his shift was a different race but there was no tension among everyone. It eventually led to a point where they could all say whatever they wanted to each other, and they laugh about many things. And this was when Thomas would begin to pull pranks at work. When someone new showed up, the supervisor told him to take the trash out while Thomas went out the side door and jumped in the dumpster. They told one guy to watch out for the raccoons because they were some mean sons of bitches. The guy cautiously went out the door, looking all over as Thomas held the lid to the trash bin slightly open. As he approached the container, Thomas jumped up, pushing the cover wide open. The guy threw the garbage bag in the air and yelled, "Oh Shit," as he ran back towards the building. Everyone laughed about that night for a long time. All hecould say to Thomas was that he was a "Sick Bastard" as he laughed about it himself.

That fall, Thomas was introduced to another guy, who had just come in and was also from Michigan. After talking a while, they discovered they only lived about an hour away from each other. They ended up working on the same shift and became good friends. The pranks continued as they took things to the next level. He covered Thomas in toothpaste one night after he had passed out in a chair from drinking. Thomas retaliated when they worked together a few days later. Thomas brought the trash out one day and also brought the hole puncher with him. Thomas emptied the paper into his vents and turned his air conditioning on high. He went back in and set up a ride with one of his other coworkers. At shift change, they jumped in the car and waited for him to come out. He sat down with the door open and cranked his car up as it began to snow paper clippings in his vehicle, landing everywhere, including into his hair. The race was on to get back to the dorm. Thomas's raced to his apartment in the same fashion he did as a child when his father crumbled into a ball at the door when he went to swat Thomas. Thomas again made it to his apartment just in time. That turned out to be a short-lived prank war.

Thomas visited his family during the holidays, and the change in weather made Thomas sick. He was only there for a short time, but he could not enjoy those moments with family. Thomas could not wait to get back to the warmer weather. He returned to home and ended up on sick for a few days. He recovered quickly and brought in the New Year at a large party thrown by people he worked with. The coming year was going to see many changes coming for him.

Memorable Moments

At the beginning of the year, Thomas and his friends watched as Communist countries crumbled like Yugoslavia and Czechoslovakia. Yugoslavia dissolved into the small nations of Slovenia, Croatia, Bosnia-Herzegovina, Serbia. War had broken out between the Serbs, Croats, and Bosniaks. They wondered if this would be the next spot that the United States would be headed to.

That year, the winter of that year saw Thomas and a friend traveling across the south as his favorite band had released a new album the previous year. U2 had released the album, Achtung Baby. The tour was to kick off at the Lakeland Civic Center. Thomas again bought his tickets through their magazine Propaganda, and the seats were not disappointing. They landed tickets for the floor, about fifteen rows back. It was the first album released by U2 in many years. After the Rattle and Hum album, they took time off to dream it all up again. During their time off, they did release a few songs, which were remakes of older music like Cole Porters Night and Day.

The tour was dubbed Zoo TV. Loads of TV monitors with satellite feeds to coincide with the music. After the opening song Zoo Station, Bono clicked through various channels showing politicians arguing, evangelists preaching, commercials, clips as He said, "What is this shit." "You didn't come here to watch TV now, did ya?" And they broke out into the song Even better than the real thing. The concert was electrifying, and there was so much to take in. As they played his favorite song, The Fly, Thomas watched in amazement as words flashed across the screen. Words and phrases such as Everything you know are wrong, Everyone is a racist, Watch more TV, Bomb, Sex, A liar won't believe in anyone else, Believe, It's your world you can change it. It brought new meaning to older songs too. Lyrics to the song Bullet The Blue Sky speak of people burning crosses and seeing the flames higher and higher. On the screens, the image of burning crosses morphed into a Swastika as Bono sang, "Don't let it happen again." Thomas also bought tickets to the concert the following night in the Miami Area. He and his friend drove home that night and then hit the road the following afternoon to take in the next show, and it was just as great as opening night. The two nights of music left Thomas on a natural high, which lasted for some time.

At one point during the spring, Thomas and his friends went camping and they only camped for a few days. The first night, they had a fire with many drinks. Thomas passed out early but woke up to his friends trying to pick him up. They were going to bring him out into the woods and leave him there. He stayed up after that and, at one point, venturing into the woods with one person leading the charge. Everyone was on edge for fear of running into a Banana Spider web. A Banana Spider is three inches long. They did not come across any much to Thomas's delight. The next day they headed to natural springs where they could view the Manatees. It was a memorable time for Thomas.

Later that spring, Thomas found himself in the Turks and Caicos. A friend from school was teaching there as part of her college program. She had a place to stay; all he needed was a plane ticket and spending money. The flight to the only cost $175 round trip, and he ended up on the same flight with Spud Webb, who at the time was one of the NBA's shortest players at 5'7". He was disappointed because he was unable to get his autograph. Thomas's friend met him at the airport, and they were escorted back to where she and her other classmates were staying. Thomas spent a week there and enjoyed every minute of it. She made sure they had plenty to do, and some of the highlights were going on the Booze Cruise onto a private island. The light blue water and the warm ocean breeze made it one of the most enjoyable times Thomas had in the military. Drinking local beer and soaking up all the sun he could while he was there. Thomas took a liking to the native beer of the islands, and ended up buying a bottle of Dom Perignon which they drank from coffee cups at the villa. Thomas dreamed of one day returning to the islands to be married. The week went by too fast, and Thomas had to return to home. The coming months would see many changes to his life.

During the summer, he would meet someone who would change his life. A southern girl. They met while talking on the phone at work during daily exercises that were conducted. They clicked immediately and were inseparable until she was transferred to the mid-west, and he stayed where he was. Thomas was being transferred to Austria. They spent countless hours talking on the phone. At night when the temps dropped, he would bring his blanket with him. They could not control the air, and the hours spent talking would lead him to be cold. They joked about how he was Linus, and she was Sally from the Peanuts comic strip. Thomas ended up making two trips to visit her. She had a son with whom Thomas had grown close.

In December of that year, he visted her again and it was just before he headed back to his home town to visit his parents. Thomas had to return at the beginning of January. They talked of marriage and began to look at rings before he left. While in Ohio, they spoke on the phone as much as possible, He left his parents house after the New Year and and was headed to Europe.

Slipping Into A Dark Place

Arriving at the airport, Thomas settled in for the long delay for his flight overseas. He listened to music on his Walk-Man radio. He could only bring a few tapes as there was not much room on the flight. He left that evening on his flight, nervous and anxious, not knowing what to expect when he arrived. He dosed on and off several times as his flight crossed the Atlantic Ocean en route the first stop. The flight landed in the early hours of the morning; the sun had just begun to rise in the distance. They were given enough time to stretch, goto the bathroom. and were given a quick meal. The meal consisted of a ham sandwich with a roll. Some chips and chocolate are made in Switzerland. He stomached down as much as he could, knowing this was it until they reached the next destination, which was Italy. On the flight, they played a movie in which he enjoyed Honeymoon in Vegas. At the end of the film, he was surprised to hear a song by his favorite singer. The music was that of Elvis Presley but sung by various artists. Bono of U2 sung Can't Help Falling in Love. A version he still loves to this day. Upon arriving at their refueling spot and stepping off the plane, he realized the Alps Mountain range was around them. The snow-capped mountains captivated him as he thought back to all the history that had taken place where he was walking.

The area he went to near Aviano air base and was built in 1911 and served as a training base until World War 1 when they began to fly missions against the Austro-Hungarian and German armies. The Austro-German troops captured the base. In between the wars, the base was again used for training purposes. During World War 2, the Italian Air force and German Luftwaffe flew many missions from that location until British forces captured the base, and it was eventually turned back over to the Italian government in 1947. Thomas could picture in his mind Luftwaffe pilots scrambling to their Messerschmitt BF-109's like a report of British Spitfires were en route. Thomas also took in as much of the scenery as he could. Not being able to take pictures, he enjoyed the view. Thinking of how vast the mountain range was as it stretched as far north as France and Germany. They soon reboarded the flight and the final leg to Austria. It was dark when they landed in Austria. There was an 6-hour difference in time from when he started in the United States. Thomas fell into a deep sleep feeling overwhelmed by the last few days.

Things were going smoothly for Thomas until he called his fiance one night and another man answered the phone half asleep. Thomas was heartbroken and it sent him into a depression.

He started to drink more frequently and being away from everyone made things more difficult. Thomas stayed only a few more months and then headed back to the States

When Thomas departed back to the continental U.S. The flight itinerary back was different than before, with his first stop being in Germany and a layover for the night. It again excited him, knowing he was in another country rich in history. The flight arrival timing and an early departure did not leave him time to explore, so he quickly fell asleep, knowing the next day was the longest of his journey.

The next day upon arrival at Stateside and another long day, he stopped at a bar in the airport and enjoyed some food that he had craved for so long. He arrived back in his hometown later that evening and could not sleep because of the time change.

He spent most of the night awake, trying to get settled. Falling asleep in the early hours of the morning and awaking to chaos as his mother found a pack of cigarettes that he had. And like every mother, he was lectured, but he continued.

That fall, he started taking college courses again and moving onto the next stage of his life. He was excited to be starting something new and being around his hometown. He reunited with his childhood friend, who had also returned from the service and took classes at the exact location.

A Fresh Start

In the spring of 1994, Thomas spent taking classes, and on the weekends, he and his friend would hit the local bar to unwind from a week's worth of lessons. Thomas met up with another childhood friend and they reconnected. His girlfriend was related to someone Thomas had grown up with. This was thru marriage. For a few years, they would help each other out with various things. They considered each other family. They would laugh as they went out to stores, and Thomas would stall out in his standard vehicle, which he was still learning to drive.

As spring turned to summer Thomas and his friend heading to the bar 3 nights a week. Thursday thru Saturday. No one knew, but Thomas was still dealing with issues from his time overseas. Sleepless nights for months were catching up with him, but he continued to forge ahead. Before they would hit the bar, they would watch comedy to get geared up for the night. They developed their own language out of moments from the movies and shows they watched. They could stand directly behind or in front of someone at the bar and talk about them laughing. The people would have no clue what was going on, and they referred to them as the two old guys on the Muppet's in the balcony. The nights at the bar, there would be local women they were in school with. One night, his friend egged Thomas on to go make a girl's jaw drop, and of course, Thomas was ready for a good laugh and followed suit. She was stunningly beautiful, and under any other circumstances, Thomas would not have approached her. But with the beer muscles on and the words already on his mind, he went for the kill. She was petite, and she was talking to someone as Thomas approached her and whispered a few things in her ear. Her jaw dropped to the floor. Thomas's friend had taken a drink at the same time and was spewing beer everywhere. For a few years after that night, whenever they met, she would recall that moment and laugh. They went out a few times after that on their own. Thomas was not drinking as much at the time, and again he could not find the words to say. She eventually ended up married with a few children. Also, that summer, Thomas said goodbye to his maternal grandfather. A few years before, he was placed into a nursing home. His grandfather, after having the stroke, became quite a character. Unable to speak and with limited mobility, he would make his way around the building. Having coffee with the workers. He became lighter and gentler. At the funeral, pallbearers were picked, including Thomas and his friend during his high school years.

That fall, as classes started up, Thomas found it harder to concentrate, and the issues remained. His grades continued to drop. He and his friend continued to hit the bars, but Thomas had met someone and was in a relationship with her for a short time. Thomas didn't go out as often, and his friends joked about it. They would say, "Just add Thomas, and you have a family." Thomas laughed, but he didn't find humor in it. She had a young son, so they would stay in. Thomas became restless, and they broke up. He wanted to be with his friends.

Falling Down

Thomas was slipping into a dark place this time. Things continued to go downhill for him and he dropped out of college. The events of being overseas weighed heavily on him.

By summer, with encouragement from his parents, he sought help. He dealt with those issues for months, and by the onset of winter, he was coming back around. Very few people knew of what he dealt with, and he wanted it to remain that way. Those that did know understood what was going on. But there was still an issue with him. Something he could not figure out. Some things did not make sense to him. Recurring childhood memories like his parents talking to someone at their kitchen table telling their friends that they had to fire the babysitter because when they arrived home, Thomas had a black eye. And the babysitter stated he had fallen out of the stroller. He often wondered why he kept having this memory pop up in his mind, but he never pursued answers.

That summer, he went outside to have a cigarette after waking up from nightmares. His father had taught him to put the butts between the deck boards, and that was precisely what he did. This time though, that cigarette started to smolder with piled-up leaves under the porch. The local fire department was called, and the thought was the smoke was coming from the neighbor's boat that was parked in the driveway. They pulled out the stairs and noticed what was happening, and put out the smoldering leaves. Thomas and his friend laughed about that for many years later.

During that winter, he asked his parents if he had been abused as a child, and they looked upon him as though he had two heads. He shrugged it off and went on with his life. He would wake up some nights feeling like he was back overseas and unable to get back into a deep sleep.

A New Love

By spring, Thomas landed a job at a local store. With the help of his uncle, who also worked there. He found his motivation again, and life was improving for Thomas. He worked the overnight shift, and it was mainly on weekends. He was hanging out with his friends and having fun. There was a regular group that he hung out with, and then another joined the group. Thomas thought she was breathtaking as he sat in a booth across from her. Captivated by her beauty and hanging on every word she spoke, they started to become friends. His time off was spent with her as they became really good friends. She had the look of Elaine Benes from Seinfeld, and the group often stated that.

As time went on, their friends encouraged both to try dating each other. She was just a few months removed from an abusive relationship and was hesitant about proceeding, but they gave it a go. Thomas was on cloud nine, and their friends kept saying what a cute couple they made. They took things slow, which was what both of them wanted. Once in a while, they would go out with their friends dancing. After dancing the night away, they sat at a table one night at a club, and she laid back in his arms. Thomas had to remind himself to breathe as this beauty rested her head against his chest. She eventually had met his parents, and everyone thought highly of her. He had also met her parents, and things were going well. One evening watching television, she laid her head on his lap. He eventually gave her a back massage, and shortly thereafter, they kissed for the first time. He viewed her as a goddess, but his insecurities raced in his mind. What did someone so painstaking beautiful see in him? He was falling for her, and there was no stopping it.

As May approached, things became strained between the two. She was having a hard time dealing with the issues of her previous relationship. She ended up telling Thomas that things were not going to work. She was not ready for another relationship. Thomas understood but at the same time, he was devastated. Though the words were never spoken between them, Thomas had fallen in love with her. The heartache he felt lasted for seemed like an eternity for him. In his mind, Thomas began to wonder what was wrong with him. Thomas convinced himself that he was the reason for the breakup, and he played the what-if game in his head. He submerged himself into work to heal himself.

That summer, he helped his father build a deck for the pool in the backyard to keep occupied. As Thomas brought tools back to the house one evening, his father yelled that he thought a board would fit on the deck. He proceeded to put the board down and had to jump on it to make it work. Thomas watched as his father sprang 3 feet in the air and performed the nutcracker on a beam. Thomas asked his father if he was ok and he grumbled that he was. Thomas walked into the house and could not stop laughing. It was no laughing matter to his father as he had a dinner plate-sized bruise on his inner thigh. It could have been much worse. Thomas kept himself busy that summer between work and then rebuilding the front porch of his parent's house. His mind still wandered back to his ex from time to time. He missed her dearly. Towards the completion on the front porch, his father decided to work on the rails as Thomas finished closing in the bottom portion. His father had worked that hot summer day and was extremely tired, but he wanted to get things done. Thomas's mother sat in her rocker on the porch as they worked. His father had a temper but would never hit a woman. As his father attempted to figure out the angle to put the rail at, his mother kept nagging him. Saying, "That does not look right." "Wait till Pete comes, and he can help you." The final straw for his father was when she uttered the words, "Why don't you wait? You don't know what you are doing." His father, sweating, extremely tired threw the board in the driveway. He went upstairs, turned on the air, and didn't come down until the next day. Again, all Thomas could do is laugh, thinking not one guy in America could not relate to that situation.

Later that summer, his father had a heart attack while working in addition to the house to repair a pipe for an outside faucet. He ended up having open-heart surgery, and they opened the blockage. Upon returning home, his stubborn father stated that he was going to sleep upstairs. The doctors did not want him to do that, and he was told to stay down. As soon as he walked in, he headed for the stairs with his mother, yelling for Thomas's help. Thomas laughed and stood in front of his father and told him, "You have to get past me first, and with the shape, you are in, that is not going to happen." His father sat in the chair for the rest of the day with a defeated look on his face.

Towards late fall, with his father feeling better and having always been a hard worker, he wanted to put up some siding on the house. Thomas put the ladders up, and they took their time. They soon quit after the feet of the ladder his father was on started sliding on the deck with the upper half ratcheting down the wall. The only thing that stopped the ladder was the deck rail. His father stated, "We're done for the day. I don't need another heart attack."

WITHOUT A VOICE

In the winter of this year, Thomas had to say goodbye to someone he was not ready to say goodbye. His grandmother, who babysat him during his childhood years, was dying. At the hospital with other family in the room, he had no words to describe what he was feeling and had a tough time trying to say things to her while still coherent. She was weak from years of dealing with asthma and heart issues. A piece of him died along with her. A void that could never be refilled.

After his grandmother's funeral, he slipped even further into depression. Life was falling apart for him. Running low on money, he continued to drink and party. He maintained his job, though one night, after getting done with an evening shift, he was jumped in the parking lot because two intoxicated males did not like the jacket he was wearing. Charges were filed, but the damage was done. He was jumped from behind and repeatedly kicked, leaving a boot print on his face. From then on, he was nervous working at night. For a few months after that, he would carry a knife with him if he was working outside at night. Always looking behind him and what was going on around the area.

An Upward Trend

That summer, he spent some time camping at local campgrounds and enjoying the short time between seasons. He still dreamed of returning south, where things went so well for him. He always enjoyed the warm weather. The sun and the water, being at one with nature.

Also That summer, his sister had returned for a short stay. Still not close to her and the majority of the time jealous. He would cook meals for his parents, and no matter how hard he tried, he could not get the approval he sought and so desperately wanted. The meals he cooked his mother would not like, and in Thomas's mind, if his sister had cooked that meal the same way he had, it would have been the best meal his mother ever had. Hate and anger grew within Thomas as these moments continued. By this time, his sister was married, and she was visiting by herself. One evening, he asked about a recurring thought that kept popping into his mind at the dinner table one evening. He kept having a memory of having to hurry up and clean up the upstairs, which was in disarray. A female voice he remembered saying, hurry up before your sister gets home. Lights were on, and the bed was unmade with dresser drawers open. The voice was not that of his mother. Each time he thought of this, it gave him an uneasy feeling. Like the house had been broken into, and he asked that question without getting into further detail. And again, they had no clue what he was talking about. Thomas again shrugged off the thought.

During a family gathering, Thomas was sitting with his parent's dog on his lap. He lit a cigarette with a stick match and proceeded to put the match out in his mouth, blowing the smoking out. Thomas's mother looked at him and stated. "Don't do that in front of her. You're going to give her ideas." All Thomas could do is laugh as he imagined the dog in the house trying to strike a match.

Memorable Year

The beginning of this year was one of transformation for Thomas. The winter of this year brought a significant storm to the area he lived in. Power outages caused by fallen trees wreaked havoc near his home. The storm system stalled out for days, and everything came to a standstill. The area was shut down and progress remained slow for the following weeks.

As May approached, someone would come into Thomas's life to bring him his greatest joy yet show him some of the darkest days. Thomas had been promoted at work, and by this time, he was working as a mechanic. He felt good, looked good, and that radiated into the rest of his life. He still lacked confidence with women and, at the time, still had lingering thoughts of and what might have been with the woman he still had feelings for. A woman started frequently coming into the shop, and day by day, they talked more. They eventually started dating and seeing each other daily. He had mentioned to a friend that they were dating, and she warned him against doing so. Thomas, not having the confidence and self-esteem, ignored her advice. He was tired of being alone, and he enjoyed the companionship. There were many good times in the beginning. Thomas attempted to cook a meal for her, which ended up in disaster. Cooking the same meal his father had cooked years before chicken and dumplings. Thomas turned on the wrong burner and melted a plastic Tupperware lid that was resting on it. The smell made the meal unbearable, yet he tried.

Around the middle of June, while at his girlfriends place, Thomas received a call from his mother that his female friend had been calling for him. He knew she was looking for help, and he said he would touch base with her. His girlfriend overheard the conversation and inquired about it. Thomas told her that his female wanted help and he would deal with it later. She took it to the next level and thought that there was something more to it. As much as he tried to explain that nothing was going on, she never let go of that. At the time, with Thomas's low self-esteem, he accepted it for what it was known later: her issue, not his. He was growing closer to her and her son. As the summer moved on, they spent more and more time together, enjoying many moments.

Later that summer, he and and his girlfriend were on the way to the store. Thomas stared out the window, being tired. As they passed by the street that his female friend lived on, she angrily asked, "Is she there?" Thomas shook his head in disgust and sighed. Things improved over the coming months with improvements in their relationship. By late fall, he was staying there regularly. Thomas found out soon, though, that she was chatting with other guys, which angered him, but they smoothed things over. With his low self-esteem, he continued on. One "friend" that she talked to and assured Thomas that he was just a family friend. He noticed that when there was an argument between them, her friend was around more, or she sought him out. He referred to Thomas as her "Boy toy." She told Thomas that he was a family friend who plowed her mother's driveway out in the winter. Thomas again shrugged these things off, and life continued on. The rest of this year, they continued to have up and down moments. It would be the coming year that things would yet again pose a challenge for Thomas.

Tension's Building

It took time, but things improved between Thomas and his girlfriend, and they continued moving forward. A new house was bought, and they were due to move in over the summer. The problem is that the move was taking place while Thomas was in training for a new job. When Thomas departed, he wished he could stay and help, and deep within him, Thomas wondered what else would happen while he was gone.

Thomas had known that his maternal grandmother was ill and doing well before training. That and the thought of his girlfriend hitting the bars played games with his head. A few days before the end of the training, and Thomas. He received a call on the company radio. He went to the vehicle and was given the radio, and was told his grandmother had passed. Being tired from being out in the field and thoughts running through his mind, he broke down. They gave him a moment and transported him back the company to make calls, and they arranged transportation home. He grabbed his gear and was brought right to his parent's house. She had everything settled in the new place and enjoyed the comforts. He stayed in town for the services and then headed back to training. When he arrived, they were already done training and were preparing to return home.

The rest of the year was uneventful, and life went on. He had his Christmas party with his company, but his girlfriend refused to go. He went alone and did have fun. Thomas wanted to spend more time with his friends, but it was a double-edged sword. Knowing how things had worked in the past with his girlfriend, he stayed home.

As the New Year approached, the talk was about how the computers not switching over to the Year 2000 might shut down power grids and wreak havoc with banking and stores. Programmers came up with software, and on New Year's eve, they wait and celebrated. It ended up being like any other day.

A Time of Change

Thomas and his girfriend continued to have issues. Up and down moments. At times he wanted to leave, but again, the low self-esteem and the bond he had with her son kept him there. He had grown close with her son, and he always wanted to be with Thomas. Thomas would help with homework and reading, and he would go everywhere with him. He became attached to his parents. He was a bright spot in Thomas's life. His parents eventually brought him on a trip with them to the ocean. A moment that child would never forget.

Thomas ended up taking on a new job with room for advancement. He was looking forward to the change. One of Thomas's issues was that he was transferred to evenings after training for weeks on the day shift. While at work, he often thought about what was happening at home. When he was home, he found it difficult to sleep during the day. He was always tired, and it was taking its toll on him. He maintained the house the best he could. The majority of the time, he did all the cleaning with his girlfriend pitching in occasionally. With his mother pushing him as a child to clean he could not stand any messes. His girlfriend was always obsessed with the laundry. He would ask her to pitch in, and that was her reply. I have laundry to do. He often thought, how hard is it to put in and take it out? He often thought back to his days on active duty when his friends joked about how he would make a good housewife someday. And that is just what he had become.

The Presidential Election of the year brought the two at odds. His girlfriend voted democrat and Thomas was pro-Republican. They discussed this, and he told girlfriend that the country was due for a war. It had been a long time, and the republicans would build up the military. It was an exciting election. It was also when Thomas found out he was going to be a father. He was excited but nervous about what was going to take place. When he told his parents, he thought they would be happy for him, but that was not the case. They were displeased because he had not done things the proper way. Thoughts of his childhood flashed in his head. He will never get the acceptance he so desperately wanted.

On Christmas eve of this year, they were due to go to his parents for a party. His girlfriend did not go. He went alone, and again he thought to himself he would love just one holiday or moment where it all came together. Family moments with happiness, he felt as though they just continued to evade him.

The Love of His Life

In the winter of this year, Thomas was up for more training in his job, and he planned out what he wanted to do. He planned on signing up for three more years to collect a bonus and then another three years with another bonus. The problem was that the for Thomas he would be in training when his child was due. He asked to go at a separate time, and they refused. Thomas knew he would not miss the birth of his child, and that ended his career. He would miss it but not regret that decision.

Thomas continued with his job, The midnight shift had caught up to him, and he was not getting enough sleep. As the birth of his daughter, approached the anxiety within him increased. When that day finally came, they gathered their things and went off to the hospital. He was nervous but maintained that day. He thought back to his decision to not resign from the military, and he knew he did the right thing as he cut the umbilical cord. He watched in amazement as they cleaned her up. She had jet black hair, and they joked about that, which later turned into a blonde look much like her father. The first time he held her, he looked down at her and fell in love. He was a wreck and could not stop sweating, but he could not take his eyes off her. There in front of him was a piece of him. That night he had a hard time falling asleep and eventually did and woke up late. He helped as much as he could in the coming weeks, and like any other parent, he was tired and still a nervous wreck. His girlfriend eventually had to go back to work, and this was the first night he would have to go it alone with his his daughter. It wasn't long after his girlfriend went to work, and she began to cry. He started to sweat bullets as he carried her around the room, trying to calm her down. He reached out for advice, but nothing helped. He decided to try a bottle, and they settled in the recliner. It was at that moment that all was right in the world. A tight bond had been formed as he rocked her, and she fell asleep. He eventually brought her upstairs and kissed her forehead goodnight. From that moment on, they followed the same routine day after day. That was his girl.

When September 11th came, the world changed. Thomas had just finished a late shift and settled into bed. His girlfriend woke him up at one point and told him how a plane had hit a tower. He dosed off again, and she again woke him to say to him news of the second, and he told her that is not a coincidence. He was restless the rest of the day. Eventually waking up and watching what was going on in disbelief. He thought to himself, what kind of world did he bring Ally into. Over the following days, everyone was on edge. His parents had come over for coffee and stood with his father outside, looking up at the sky and they commented on how strange it was, a sky with no aircraft overhead.

Thomas and his girlfriend were also replacing the bathroom at this time. Thomas and his father worked on it, The money mainly coming out of Thomas's pocket. The power had gone out do to an issue around of the area. Unable to work, they ended up having a block party. It was too hot to be inside, and everyone had a great time. The power came back on later that night.

Thomas enjoyed the holidays with his daughter as he thought to the future about doing all the things with her that he wanted. He enjoyed decorating for each holiday, but his girlfriend was not as enthusiastic as he was. Before his daughter was born, while he and he and his girlfriend would sit and talk, he would start singing the theme to Spongebob Squarepants as the other children watched in the living room. They were given a swing for her, and she would rock in that while things were being done. One time as she rocked in the kitchen, she began to cry hysterically as the side had come apart and she was swinging on an angle. Thomas fixed it and moved it into the living room where he was. He put her back in and placed a hat on her. Her head would get so cold from swinging. She was still restless, but then Spongebob came on the television, and she calmed down and watched. The song had calmed her down, and she eventually fell asleep. She never lost that love of Spongebob.

Tension's Mount

Many odd things began to happen in the house. The stereo would turn on by itself along with the TV. While his girlfriend would be home alone, the TV in the back bedroom would come on by itself. It made for an uneasy feeling for both of them. More things would begin to happen in the coming years.

As the seasons changed and summer approached, Thomas was laid off of work. It made for a difficult time, but they endured. He applied for many jobs with no prospects on the horizon. He was eventually called back in, but he felt that things would not improve, so he continued to look. His girlfriends son still hung tight with Thomas, and he made sure he spent time with him. The most memorable time for him was when he cut a chunk of hair in the front of his head. Thomas worked in the kitchen, and he was in the bathroom and then walked into the living room. Thomas then walked into the bathroom and found clumps of hair, and then went and looked at him. He could not stop laughing.

Thomas and his girlfriend were doing well at this time. They would sit on the couch and watch a movie, she would put her feet on his lap, and Thomas would break open the lotion and give her a foot massage. Something he enjoyed doing and became quite good at. His girlfriend was growing restless, and Thomas could sense that. They didn't have much time together alone, and he mentioned having a date night, just the two of them going out to dinner and do something. She didn't want to do that though, she wanted to go to the bars on the weekend. Thomas did not mind at first but soon grew tired of that. He was the one that would get up with the baby on those weekend mornings. And Thomas was not interested in the bar scene. He was ready for family life.

He was catching on and started to protect himself. Sliding back into that child who would lock himself in his room. The rift was beginning to grow. He ended up landing a new job with higher pay doing maintenance.

That divide grew even further apart at Christmas. Thomas always enjoyed Christmas and his ability to buy things that meant something. It wasn't easy for him at first, but he paid attention. Sometimes Thomas would have to ask what she wanted, but it eventually evolved to where Thomas didn't have to. He had a system down and stuck to it. While shopping, she would always comment on something she liked but wouldn't buy. He would take note of that and do his best to get that item if he could. When Christmas day arrived, and she opened her gift's her attitude changed quickly. He had forgotten the hat and mittens that she wanted and gave him an attitude for the rest of the day. Not talking to him, and he could feel the energy she was giving off. He had reached his limit at that point. He could no longer maintain the relationship.

Throughout the winter, strange things continued to happen in the house. This one incident sent chills through both of them. His daughters crib was in the room with a blanket covering the rail to block the light. When walking past the crib, the slightest touch or breeze would send it to the floor. In the middle of the night, they woke to the sound of a thud. Like something fell on the floor. Upon turning the light on, they noticed that their daughter was on the floor. The blanket was still on the side of the crib.

Thomas had to stop work for a while for emegency surgery. The surgery went well, and he was laid up for six weeks. A few days after, his girlfriend returned home and was throwing attitude towards Thomas. Saying he should be up and doing more. Thomas was sleeping in the chair at the time. He was doing what he could, he thought as she did the dishes and immediately went to bed. She had to help him shower at first, but he gained his strength back and managed to make it upstairs to shower on his own one day.

His mobility was not excellent as he started the water and entered the shower. The hot water felt great on his back. He had adjusted everything he needed, so he had easy access with limited turning. As he started to wash, the water turned from hot to icy cold. It startled him, of course, and he turned around and noticed that the cold water knob was utterly turned on. It sent chills up his spine. He finished and went back downstairs, not wanting to go back up after what had just happened. He returned to work, and things went back into a regular routine for him.

Thomas began cleaning up the garage area and decided to start using it as a man cave. His girlfriend supported that and then complained when he went out there. He felt he could just not win. While out shopping later that fall with his girlfriend and they ran into his parents. His girlfriend ran into some people she knew she had not seen in a long time. They asked about the guy she was with and what happened to him. She replied he was right there. And they reacted negatively about how he had changed. He was milling around and acted like he heard nothing. But in his mind, he thought if they only knew what was going on.

Time's with his Daughter

By the beginning of this year, Thomas no longer wanted to go shopping with his girlfriend. He stayed home with his daughter. And by this time, she was starting to come into her own. And in February of this year, she became very ill with a stomach bug. Thomas ended up taking time off of work to be with her. She could not keep anything down, which made Thomas very nervous. He woke up in the middle of the night to see her sitting on the end of the bed watching TV. In her hand was a plastic teacup that she used to get a drink out of. But she had milk in it, and Thomas knew what was going to happen with that. He ended up going downstairs to get her a better cup and put the milk container, which was on the floor, into the fridge. When he returned with fresh water, she began to vomit again. Thomas made sure she was cleaned up, and she settled down and fell back asleep. That morning she continued to vomit, and Thomas made an appointment with her Dr. The doctor was was the same that had diagnosed Thomas with Whooping Cough.

Whenever his daughter had gone to the doctor, she was concerned about getting shots, and on this occasion, when the doctor came out, his daughter walked up and said as she looked up 'I not get a pinch." He chuckled and brought her back with him. The doctor ended up giving her a pinch and a script for a suppository. She also told Thomas to go ahead and get her McDonalds and advised him to let her have some flat coke. That coke would settle the stomach, and she also stated that he could mix any medication with whatever drink she would have to take. Thomas thought back to his childhood and remembered all the meds he had to take, including the day his father gave him NyQuil. It would have made things much more manageable. He bought her some lunch which she enjoyed. He was nervous because her skin was a pale grey. A short time later, his girlfriend called and said the drug store could not fill the script because her insurance was not current. It cost too much to buy it outright. Thomas remembered that some suppositories belonged to brother. By this time, his daughter had again begun to vomit. He looked at the script, and it was for someone who weighed more but figured if he cut it in half, it would work. About 5 hours later, she began to bounce around like her usual self. It was a time that Thomas would not forget.

One evening as Thomas and his girlfriend were cleaning in the bedroom, they noticed that their daughter was extremely quiet. Thomas went downstairs to find their daughter on the couch watching her first movie, Monsters Inc, and it was towards the end. She was wiping tears away as she watched this. Soon after this, she started to draw the show's characters, and she fell asleep one night with a pen in hand as she was drawing Randall. Thomas was able to snap a picture of this, one he fondly looked back on.

Thomas was starting to enjoy time with his. One day she walked out of the bathroom naked from the waist down. She threw her arms in the air and stated, "Pants Gone." Thomas asked what she meant and proceeded to the bathroom, and just as she had said, they were gone. She flushed her pajama bottoms and underwear down the toilet. He laughed and said that may come back to haunt us in the future. And years later, she noted an issue, and they both laughed, wondering if that was the cause. He began to read books with her also. Her favorite was "Mr. Brown Can Moo Can You." He would read the main parts, and she got to the point where she would make the sounds. His the favorite was hearing her say, "Dibble, Dibble, Dop." And it was also around this time that he introduced her to Scooby-Doo. The Creeper was the first episode she watched, and she was hooked. Thomas would come up behind her and sound the Creeper that frightened her. It brought him back to memories of his mother coming downstairs with his father's uniforms and stocking over her head. They eventually watched every episode and ended up later getting the video games that they both played together.

He also continued to do homework with his girlfriends son, and he made sure that his daughter was also included. He made sure they bought books on things she could learn to feel welcomed and educate at the same time. Class time was always after school to get something out of the way. Thomas wanted to give them chores to help out around the house. His idea was to put a list on the fridge, and they get a set amount of money for each chore done. His girlfriend refused to follow thru and help with that, saying that it was not going to work.

Thomas and his girlfriend continued to have issues on and off, but he did the best he could know what it would be like when he left. When things were horrible, he would leave and spend a night with his parents or friends. But it was his daughter that kept him going back. She would go everywhere with Thomas, and they enjoyed each other's company.

On his daughter's birthday they noticed a trend that would carry on for many years. As everyone sang Happy Birthday to her, she would run into the living room, lay on the couch and cry. Something they could never understand. She even did so at parties for other people with her Uncle laughing and saying "It's not even your Birthday." Years later they would laugh about it with her having no clue as to why she did that.

Holding on

This year there were more of the same issues between Thomas and his girlfriend. He continued to work around the house. Her son would make various meals and leave a sink full of dishes. He would return home and find that and becoming upset, he would reach out to his girlfriend. He asked her to do something about it, but her only reply was, "Well, leave them then, and I will do them." And Thomas's reply was, "I already have them finished." It was making him angry towards her son when the issue was his girlfriend. He continued to do homework with her son and his daughter. Everything he did was not good enough for his girlfriend. He was trying to make improvements to the house. Issues with the cellar walls where mice were coming in, he patched up. Attempting to paint the edging of windows one day with black paint, the paint bucket fell off the hook on the ladder and crashed down of the ground below. The color ran down all the siding as the bucket fell against the siding and he attempted to clean up the best he could. She belittled him when she returned, echoing back to his childhood when he felt he could not do anything right with his parents. Things just became more and more strenuous on Thomas as he tried to maintain for his daughter.

Things continued to slide downhill for Thomas and his girlfriend. Her son continued to have friends over and the messes that were left behind. Thomas's paternal grandfather was ill around this time, and Thomas needed an open phone line to call. Her son instantly started using the phone when they returned home. Thomas spoke with his girlfriend and said he needed that phone to find out what was going on. His girlfriend would not take control of any issues, and it was wearing on Thomas.

That summer, her son wanted to bring their daughter for a ride in the car with her friends. When he noticed this, he asked where the car seat was. His girlfriend replied they are only going a couple of blocks. Thomas said that she was not going anywhere without that car seat. Another reason he held on as long as he could for his daughter.

It was on Christmas Eve of this year that another issue added stress for Thomas. Again her son decided that he needed to change her room and put all the furniture out in the hall. She was wandering around and tripped over the table, striking her head and leaving a large knot. Thomas wanted to throw up when he had seen that happen. He was angry because of the timing of him moving these things as everyone else was getting ready to go to his grandfather's. Things settled down, but for Thomas, it was becoming increasingly difficult.

End of The Relationship

This was the year that things began to fall apart for Thomas. His grandfather, was moved to a nursing home. Before that, Thomas would check on him every morning and night. Letting his dog out and getting him things he needed such as water, a snack, or making sure he made it to bed without issues. At night Thomas would lock up for him and return the following day. One night he had let his dog out, and as soon as that happened, the smell of skunk filled the house. They could not tell if the dog had been sprayed or not. His grandfather told him to just go and will see what happens the following day. The next morning the house still smelled horrible, and his grandfather was ill because of it. The dog had been sprayed. It had taken a few weeks to get that smell out. One moment Thomas would not forget was when he went over as his grandfather wanted something from the garage. Thomas went to the garage and then went inside. His grandfather said, "Oh, I thought it was your father out there. All I could see was the bald spot." His grandfather loved his great-granddaughter and lit up every time.

Thomas would bring his daughter over. She was attached to his hip by this point and always went. She went over with Thomas one evening, and they noticed fireflies in the backyard. They returned home and grabbed jars and her brother and chased them down. They all had fun, except his girlfriend, who thought it was non-sense. Thomas didn't care what she thought. He was making memories. Thomas had a dream of floating outside a window at his grandfather's house. There was something on the wall, but it could not be made out. When he woke from this dream, he thought of how odd it was but again shrugged it off. His daughter had woken from a slumber, and just before rising out of bed, an Earth Quake shook the house. Windows rattled, and every piece of furniture was moving, which woke everyone up. They wondered for a moment if it was an explosion but soon found out it was not. This was a rare event for this part of the country. There was no damage, but it rattled everyone's nerves.

In late spring when things became very interesting. His Girlfriend went out shopping and of course. Thomas and his daughter stayed home. It was early morning when she left. And it was about 3:30 PM when Thomas felt something was not right. He put his daughter in the vehicle, and they looked around the shopping areas. His girlfriend was nowhere to be found. He returned home and waited. When she returned home with no bags, he asked where she had been. She replied she had been down by the river. And then asked him to leave. He knew at that point that things were done between them. Thomas grabbed a few things and kissed his daughter goodbye as he went to his grandfather's and slept. He stayed there for the week. His daughter and his ex girlfriend's son were over the majority of the time.

Thomas took care of his daughter like he always had and when his girlfriend had returned, his daughter went back over. His ex had gone cycling. It continued like this into the following week. Thomas had been keeping notes. Her son spoke of how his mother was going to bring someone over. He was a nice guy. That Friday, Thomas was watching his daughter, and a knock came on the door around dusk. Her son came and spent the night. Thomas ended up feeding him and keeping him there the night. They played some video games, and the kids drifted off to sleep.

It was later the next day that Thomas decided it was time they talk. He arranged it with her, and they sat on the front porch and talked. He knew she was seeing someone. He also heard through the grapevine that she was pregnant. He wanted to see what she said. He asked if that question, and her response was no. Again knowing all the info he had and he talked about maybe trying to work things out. She replied she didn't know if they could, and he asked again if there was someone. She again responded with a no. He took a deep breath and said I'm done. She started crying and ran off into the house. He walked back and prepared for what he had to do.

Over the coming weeks, more and more issues began popping up. It was the day of his daughter's birthday, and she and Thomas made a cake together. They had a small party, and she had a few friends over. She enjoyed the day with her father. She was going to go back with her mother for the night. Her mother said she was going to have a party for her. A few days later, he returned his daughter to his ex for the weekend. As he did so, she replied, "Parties Over" "Come on," as he handed his daughter over. And as he was doing so, she reached out for her father crying. Yelling "Daddy" repeatedly as he walked away. It was and remained a moment that would haunt him for years. He was breaking down. Inside the house, he broke down in tears. She had changed for the worse and he could not figure out what was wrong. There were darker days on the horizon.......

CHAPTER 3

Mounting Turmoil

Thomas spent the next few days cleaning the house and trying to adjust to moments without his daughter. He felt sick knowing she wanted to be with him and couldn't. He tried hard to maintain for her. There were a couple of occasions where Thomas's concerns were raised. He had forgotten to bring his daughter's book bag with her, and he needed to drop it off before he left for work. She was eating her favorite meal of Pizza Rolls and was excited to see Thomas. When he arrived at the door there was a strong smell of pot. Thomas wondered if he was smoking in the house and around his daughter and raised that concern with his ex. The second time he was concerned, he was bringing her home from across the street, and as they walked towards his ex's house, he noticed her boyfriend was looking over Thomas's tools. Some of those tools were antique and were given to him when his grandmother passed. They were more of sentimental value than valuable. He wanted to remove his belongings and move forward. He spoke to his grandfather about staying in the house which he approved of.

One evening when his ex was gone, he went over to the garage and removed his property. When she found out, she was upset, telling Thomas, "You didn't even leave me any tools." His reply was, "I left you what you had when I arrived a screwdriver, wrench, and hammer."

A couple of weeks passed, and again she would not come near Thomas when she was dropped off by her brother. This time she would run away from him. He finally got her to open up to him. He held her as she cried and hugged her father.

That evening before he brought her to her mothers house, he came up with a saying that they would repeat for many years. Thomas would say, "What do we remember?" And she would reply, "Daddy loves me."

As the days passed, Thomas had an uneasy feeling about him. Paranoia was setting in. A friend of his would talk to Thomas at various times. She had met his daughter and would braid his daughter's hair one morning. Then she started warning him to watch his house, car, and back. He thought back to the moment his ex had threatened him on the front porch of her house. The paranoia was growing in Thomas, and it was taking a toll on him. He soon found out that the "family friend that plowed her mother's driveway was an ex-boyfriend. Thomas began to miss work as there was no end in sight to his downfall. His ex and her boyfriend hung out with someone from the company Thomas worked for. Thomas's work was on the decline, and he was written up for his performance.

Soon after, the pressure had gotten to Thomas as he showed up to work and could not function. A co-worker who was there to help him brought him to the hospital. Thomas's father showed up a short time later. While waiting to be brought to the floor, he broke down in tears, saying to his father that he would lose his daughter and there was nothing that could be done. Thomas spent the next couple of weeks in the hospital. The rest of the year, he spent as much time with her as possible.

That fall, he started dating another woman, this one of Italian descent. They clicked instantly and were inseparable. The more they talked, the more they fell for each other, and things progressed along at a pace that Thomas was comfortable with. Thomas spent as much time with her as he could, They raked leaves together, and Thomas would hide in them and jump out when she came close. She would yell "Don't" after being scared but would want him to do it again. It was moments like this that he wouldn't trade in for the world.

Season of Change

Thomas and his ex went to Family Court, and Thomas was pleased by the outcome despite knowing it should have been different. He didn't lose any time with his daughter and made the most of every moment. She began to give him makeover's even to the point of having his nails done. One of those evening's she painted his nails a hot pink, complete with eye shadow. The following day Thomas went to work and had to drive around the village visiting various places. Signing paperwork and collecting items to bring back to work. His last stop was at the local store to grab a drink, and as he handed the cashier his cash, he noticed that he was still wearing that hot pink nail polish. He quickly balled his hands up and left the store, laughing as he entered his vehicle.

Growing Pains

His daughter gave Thomas a run for his money as she grew older and started testing the waters on what she could get away with. She started going to the local Boy's and Girl's club with a friend, and Thomas would drop her off and pick her up. She was typically dropped off at the front door, but on this one day, in particular, she asked to drop her off down the street. Thomas thought this was odd, but he dropped her off where she requested. Thomas knew something was up and gave it about 10 minutes before returning to the club to find that she was not there. Thomas drove all over town looking at spots she would frequent and eventually found her walking down the street with more kids on the far side of town. She had seen her father coming and tried to hide behind friends, but the gig was up. Thomas was livid and scolded her for doing that. She wanted more freedom but was scared to ask. Thomas grounded her, and she was dropped off to her mother's that evening. Once back her mothers she was ungrounded. Other's noticed this and spoke to Thomas about this issue which frustrated him. How do you do it when only one parent would follow through when issues like this arise?

She loved her animals, and they loved her. Thomas had picked up two Dwarf Russian Hamsters from someone local and brought them home to her. She instantly fell in love with the tiny creatures who were about the size of her thumb. But like all living things, they soon passed on. The snow was already on the ground, and she wanted to bury them. With the ground too hard, they were placed under the snow. They were replaced by a regular hamster a few weeks later. She would take him out of the cage and let him run around. One evening while downstairs and she playing her favorite game, they heard a crash. The cat had knocked over the pen, and the hamster was under the bed. When Thomas retrieved him, his little heart was pounding, and she tried to calm him down. He was placed back in the cage, and they kept an eye on him. The following day she served him breakfast and went off to school. Shortly after that, Thomas noticed the hamster was not moving and that the stress of the previous night's incident had taken a toll on him. Thomas's father jumped into action as Thomas went to work. He scoured the county for a replacement and eventually found one. The problem was this one was bigger. His father did not want to see her go through another loss like the previous two and brought it home. When she returned from school, she commented on how much bigger he became since school. Thomas told her, "With the amount of food you feed him, it's no wonder." For weeks she wondered if they were going to need a more giant cage.

Every Christmas, it was the same routine for Thomas and his daughter. They both liked to decorate the house with a mix of white and colored lights. Thomas loved to decorate and would do so for every Holiday as his parents did for him and his sister when they were young. They would make cookies like Peanut Butter Blossoms, Sugar cookies with frosting on them, and even Reindeer cookies with pretzel pieces for antlers. He would make these for her Christmas parties at school or try and come up with something unique that she could help him with. They would make a Gingerbread house, and if Thomas could not afford it, they would use graham crackers to build it. Elf on the shelf was another thing he would use. Every Christmas, she would ask if she could stay Christmas eve, but it was worked out that she would be returned to her mom. The first Christmas after the breakup, Thomas had her for the night. They opened their gifts, and then she would leave for her mom's. Thomas ended up going back to bed and sleeping the day away. She didn't have time to play and enjoy any of her gifts. He decided that he would pick her up on Christmas day and spend time with her and enjoy the rest of the day.

Change

Once again, Thomas was changing jobs, and this time it was not of his own doing. The company he worked for was moving to Mexico, so he started looking for a new job. A test Thomas had taken for a better job had come back and scored well on it, but he would have to wait. He started to collect unemployment, which was going to be a challenge, but he trudged on. She said to her father that she wished her mother would spend more time with her. Thomas reached out to her but his pleas went unheard.

It was February, and Thomas learned that he had an interview for the position he tested for. This interview would change his and his daughter's life if he were to land it. Thomas was interviewed later that spring, and by summer, Thomas began to work at a local nursing home. He loved the job, and training was intense at times, but he made it through and later that summer. His confidence was high, but his self-esteem was still low, and his weight was the heaviest Thomas had ever seen. He worked the midnight shift to sleep during the day while she was at school, and if she had an appointment, he could take her to it. He loved to help people, and this job allowed him to do just that.

She continued to do poorly in school, and yet again, the teachers and staff continued to push her along. Around this time, she began to ask her father if he could buy gifts so she could give them to her mother. Thomas did what he could, but he could not do it as much as he wanted. Years later he learned that she did this to get her mothers attention. To feel the gratitude and love she longed for.

Her favorite cat had passed away after it was struck by a car, and she was found in a snowbank along the side of the road. She was heartbroken, and a few days later, her grandfather returned with a new cat. They had a bond that could not be broken.

Awkward Moments

Thomas had picked up Ally from school one afternoon, and on his way home, she began to talk to her father about what she had been up to. She proceeded to tell Thomas that her mother said not to say anything because it would make him mad, and Thomas assured her that things would be fine. At that moment, Thomas was not ready to hear what came out of her mouth as she began to him about having sex and getting into detail. Thomas could not un-hear this and wanted to puncture his eardrums but let her go on as he knew this was a moment that she was opening up, and he wanted her to feel comfortable in doing so. As he white-knuckled the steering wheel, he took a deep breath and said, "Alright, lets make you an appointment?" Thomas made an appointment as soon as they arrived home.

Thomas had mentioned this to his parents, and moments after walking away, his mother picked up the phone and started calling everyone. The same thing she had done years prior with Thomas. This embarrassed her and Thomas argued with his mother over this, knowing how it made him feel when he was a child.

That Christmas, Thomas could see that childhood moment of his come into play at a family Christmas gathering. Many in the family thought that he was catering to her, which he was not. If they only knew how he felt as a child, they would understand what she was going through.

The Accident

His daughter continued to have issues with schoolwork and not wanting to go. Crying and pleading at times for Thomas and her mom not to make her go. The principal of the school continued to insist it was Thomas and her mom not being strict enough.

Anyone who Thomas dated and she met, she would ask if they would be her mom. Each one saying they would be there for him and each one not following through, sometimes through no fault of their own. She continued to ask her father to buy things for her mom. She also became so obsessed with it that she would wrap anything to give it to her mom.

She was never one for Halloween, and it continued. She would not want to go onto porches, and eventually, Thomas quit taking her.

It was December, and his parents went shopping for Christmas as they had done many years prior. A vehicle crossed the center line on the return trip, causing his parents to hit the car and careen off into a snow piled ditch. Airbags were deployed, and luckily nobody was hurt seriously.

As everyone was opening gifts on Christmas Day, Thomas's father had a slur to his speech. But a short time later, that slur had disappeared. The rest of the day went on without incident, and they enjoyed the day. It was in the weeks to come that things would drastically change.

Loss and Heartache

Thomas's father was attempting to make meatballs for a Spaghetti dinner, but he encountered a problem, he could not form a meatball with his hand. As he sat on the couch trying to explain what had happened, he suddenly stopped talking and stared straight ahead. He resumed talking, and they tried to speak to him about it; he became frustrated, not knowing what was going on. He was brought to the hospital, and a few hours later, his father was informed he had a mass on his lung. He was shipped to a larger hospital for further tests. After arriving, they took him off all medications so they could perform a biopsy. Once doing so, the fluid built up in his father's lungs, making it difficult for him to breathe. Sending him into Congestive Heart Failure.

That night Thomas and his mother spent the first of many nights in a Hotel room close by the hospital. His mother started to place calls to the family as Thomas flipped through the channels on the Television set. He listened as she explained what was going on but moments later puzzled Thomas as mentioned procedures that had not been done. He thought to himself, "Where did this come from?" After she entered another room to change, he dialed a family member from each side and told them that he would pass along the info because what she had said did not happen. He also told them to not pass along any information until they have heard from Thomas.

The biopsy revealed he had Stage 3 and 4 Cancer. Thomas tried to help him the best that he could go forward to include taking him to appointments and helping him shave his head. Many moments where he was rushed to the hospital with Thomas holding his father up, trying to prevent him from cracking his head on an object in a tight space. Pleading with his father to squeeze his hand to see if there was a response, his father did.

That March, he lost another person he had a connection with. His Uncle passed away from heart failure. Complications from years of being on dialysis finally took a toll on him. He thought back to his childhood and all the fun times they had together. It was a loss that weighed heavily on him, but he did not show it. A loss of a brilliant man who could have made a difference in the world.

While at the hospital, Thomas would go have coffee with him after work in the morning. One morning when he arrived at the hospital, his father yelled at him for not being there sooner. He complained about the internet being down, and he could not figure it out. Thomas walked out to the nurse's station and talked to them, explaining what he had said. Moments later, he walked in and told him it was fixed. Thomas laid down later that morning and cried himself to sleep. Soon after, he was brought home and placed under Hospice Care.

Frail and bedridden, when Thomas's uncles showed up his father lit up like no issues were going on. They spent the day talking and reminiscing, and when it was time for the last brother to leave, he turned to Thomas's father and said, "I will see you tomorrow." And his father replied, "No, you won't, I won't be here." He then turned to Thomas and uttered, "Take care of your mother." Thomas told him he would comfort him.

That night his father was restless, and Thomas slept on the couch next to him. Thomas tried to comfort him the best that he could. His father said to Thomas, "I wish we could have been closer." And the only words that could come out of Thomas's mouth were "I know." He told his father it would be alright and to try and rest.

Thomas's sister showed up that day to relieve Thomas, who was exhausted and needed plenty of rest. That evening they began to give him morphine to ease the restlessness. The following day family sat in the living room around him. His granddaughter sat on one side, holding his hand the entire time. Thomas sat on the other side, dabbing at the fluid that was slowly enveloping him. It sounded as though he was calling out to his wife and for his granddaughter, who brought him so much joy. Within a few hours, the spark that light the flame of his life had burnt out. Thomas felt as though everything rested on his shoulders now.

That summer, Thomas had picked up his daughter from the Boy's and Girl's Club and noticed that on her arm were cut marks. Thomas wanted to take her to counseling and inquired about it since she had difficulty dealing with her grandfather's death. When this was brought to her moms attention, she did not think she needed to go, and with the laws in place, both parents had to consent. She didn't go.

That fall, she started Middle school, and her grades once again were beginning to suffer. Thomas called the school after the first report cards came out and a meeting was set up. He was encouraged by his girlfriend at the time to do so. It took months of testing, but it was finally revealed that she was learning disabled, and it took some time for her to see the progress she made, but it was worth it.

His daughter wanted to dye her hair all the time, and the go-to color was the dark color of her mother and brothers. Her grandmother would always comment that her natural color was so much better.

By the end of the year, Thomas had moved out into the country. He and his daughter liked it, and she was still around him a lot. They had a cat and the cat would scratch the hell out of Thomas and then want to cuddle. That Christmas was different than those of the past when his father was around. Some changes are complex, and others are good. This was the beginning of a very dark cycle for Thomas.

Feeling like a Failure

Things were getting more and more strenuous on Thomas. His mother would tell him that his father would be disappointed in him for not taking care of her as he asked. Thomas would get angry and hang up on her. Often breaking down crying afterward, feeling like a failure for not living up to those expectations. Thoughts of his childhood and wanting that acceptance from his parents flashed through his mind. She was demanding so much of Thomas, and he wanted to fulfill his dying father's request, but it was taking a toll on him. If he didn't do as she said, she would tell people he was on meth or doing drugs. Thomas had his hands tied with his daughter. He and his sister were still in communication at this point and trying to figure what, if anything, they could do. Thomas often wished his father was still around as he was the glue that kept everything together all those years. He knew why his father kept smoking all those years. His mother never understood why his father had to go to the store so much. After his retirement, it was a trip he often took several times a day to get away and breathe.

His Daughter's Dilemma's

His daughter was having issues with other kids at school and often spoke to her father about these. All she wanted was to be liked by everyone, and Thomas gave her the hard truth. Not everyone would be her friend, and you don't need many friends to be truly happy. Everyone has their best friend and someone they can rely on, and that is what truly matters.

Thomas taught her about boys and how they treat girls at that age. How they think and what their intentions are. He gave her the best advice that he could still she longed for a mother figure to go to for this kind of advice. When she tried to talk to her mom, she was given short answers or felt ignored.

That summer, Thomas had to take time away from work because his ex had taken off to Chicago. His daughter contacted her father on a Friday night because she was nervous and didn't want to be alone. The anxiety of school issues bringing her to tears.

Things started to become heated again as another girl from school joined in and added to issues earlier in the year. They would walk by the house, raising her fears and anxieties. By this time, her mother had taken off on multiple trips around surrounding states. This next trip brought things to a new level. His daughter and her boyfriend spoke of how they would stay at her brothers house to watch the dog. They had asked her boyfriend to remain so she would not be alone. Her boyfriend wanted to mention this to Thomas beforehand because he knew it would not fly with Thomas. Again he took the weekend off and had her bring the dog over to his place. Trying to work, issues with his daughter and mounting pressure from his mother took a toll on Thomas.

That Thanksgiving, his daughter came to Thomas after not feeling included in her mother's. She felt that numerous times before as everyone would play a game, and it was something that she didn't know how to play and not having a room at the table.

Thomas again started to have more vivid dreams than he remembered. One was driving at night, down a highway in the rain, and then an area with a lot of smoke or fog and many people milling around a building with multiple cars. The second dream was more straightforward, and he was outside a large building at night in a parking lot filled with cars.

Thomas's mother was relentless about things she could not control. He soon spoke to her doctor, and he mentioned her showing signs of other issues. The tunnel Thomas was traveling down was getting darker and darker.

The Tunnel Deepens

The spring of 2018 saw significant changes coming in Thomas's way. He lost the job that he loved and started beating himself up for doing so daily. He left behind many people that he became close to and considered family. He began to feel like an outsider.

The issue his daughter had at school had been remedied by this time. She understood now. Thomas was still having issues with his mother, and she did not know that he and his sister had been talking and comparing notes. Her matters were coming to light for them. Around this time, his mother mentioned to him that his sister was having marital problems because his sister was not talking to her about anything personal. This was completely false as he remembered his father telling him not to tell his mother that he was taking medication for cholesterol. She would make it out to be that he needed surgery to have his arteries cleaned out. Thomas and his sister thought, if she is saying this to us, what is she saying to other people. Thomas was making plans to leave the area, and he was taking his daughter with him. They both needed a fresh start.

In the meantime, Thomas's mother called anyone and everyone to find out what was going on. She heard he was moving and called his landlord and former employment for further information. She never called Thomas to ask. When she did speak to Thomas, she said, "You lied to me; you didn't say you were seeing someone." And on top of that, Thomas was seeing someone from his past. The same one he fell in love with back in the early days. His ex had a going away party for their daughter, and Thomas's mother was invited. Thomas knew he had to get away from his mother as she was becoming toxic. She showed up at his door the night before Thomas left, but he was at a loss for words. He left without saying goodbye.

    A few days later, Thomas, his daughter, and her boyfriend headed south in the early morning hours packed with clothes and a fractured family tree. It was towards nightfall that they decided to spend the night. They headed toward Roanoke, Virginia, to spend the night. They stopped at a rest area, and Thomas stepped out of the car to smoke. As he gazed at the traffic going by, he had that strangely familiar feeling he had seen this before. As they finished the final 35 miles to Roanoke, it became darker, and rain began to fall. Thomas remembered the dream, and it sent chills through him. He noticed a sign for rest are and decided to stop and regroup. As he pulled off the road, it struck him again, this was his dream, and it was not smoke or fog. It was clouded from being in the mountains. The rest area was packed full of people pulled off the road, with many people going in and out of the rest area bathroom. He knew then that he had dreams of his future. After a brief stop, they moved on.

    They eventually reached the outskirts of Roanoke and stopped at their Hotel. Thomas jumped out and lit a cigarette, the goosebumps and hair raised on his arms as this was the building in his dreams. He could not believe what was happening. They settled in for the night, for they were to rise early to finish the trip. Thomas always loved traveling, and his daughter was enjoying it as well. While driving through the mountains and along the coast, they would stop at various places to snap photos, including state lines.

    Later that night, they met up with his girlfriend, and the first few days went well. They talked about finding work and the steps needed to move forward. A school was located for his daughter. Things were going well, or so Thomas thought. He thought her boyfriend was applying for jobs when in fact, he was not. He had been playing on his daughters fears about snakes and spiders. Thomas confronted him about this and asked him," You have no intention of getting a job, do you?" And his reply was," Your right, I'm not going to lie about it." He had been talking to his daughters mom the whole time and had no intentions of staying in the south He told him to walk away because he needed space. A while later, there was another confrontation between Thomas's girlfriend and and her boyfriend. Thomas talked her out of sending him down the road with his bags as they were leaving north the next day. Thomas remained quiet on the way to the airport. He watched the plane take off and had no clue when he would see his daughter again again.

Thomas was becoming depressed, and things were going downhill. Then more issues began to arise. He had been applying for jobs and working around the house. One afternoon while repairing the water heater, the power went out, which is not unusual for the south. But this was not because of a storm; this was because his girlfriend didn't pay the bill. A short time later, he found out that she had not paid the taxes either, which she told Thomas she had paid before going down. Thomas ended up paying for these, and he needed a new vehicle, but in exchange, she let him use one of her vehicles. A couple of weeks later, the central air went out, and again Thomas covered that bill.

Eventually, he ended up working for a manufacturing company. It didn't last long as he could not keep pace with the work and issues with his vision. He needed Bi-focals but could not get adjusted to the position. Add in the fact that before Thomas starting that job, he knew he would be paying child support, and when the notice came due, he had asked his girlfriend about getting a part-time job. She stated before going down that she would, but when the time came, she refused.

Thomas had been talking to a friend from childhood, throughout the whole ordeal. Thomas had been there for his friend when he was going through difficult times himself, and his friend knew of his family-wise issues. He teamed with another friend to get him out of that situation and to regroup. She told her friends that she didn't want him there, but before leaving, she changed her story and wanted him to return if Thomas landed the other job that he had applied for. He left and has not been back till this day.

Thomas and his friend drove back to his place, and he would help Thomas get back on his feet. He put Thomas to work, and he did the best he could to keep up. All of the events of the past year had taken a toll on him. Part of him had given up, and he wanted to end it, and most of the time, he was just depressed. He had taken to prayer by this time for assistance. He continued to beat himself up daily for losing his job. Thinking if he had done something different, he would still have his career and be around his daughter.

When he first arrived, he spoke with his friend about the corner building next to his place. How he had seen this place in a dream. A few days later, Thomas could hear an Emergency vehicle coming, and his friend was outside. As it rode past, he came in, and Thomas didn't ask what was going on. Thomas was more concerned with where it came from. His friend confirmed it came from around the corner by the building that Thomas saw when he first arrived.

When Thomas first walked out the back door, he was taken aback again as there was the courtyard he had seen in his dream in front of him. The Balcony above was there, and upon opening the door, it did not reveal the site that Thomas thought he would see. It showed a lane with a building across from it. Thomas went for a walk around the local area, and as he walked near Town Hall, he started to read the plaques. And on the plaques, he read of a Civil War battle that had taken place close by and how the Town Hall was burned down. This took place in the fields directly behind where they lived. He taught Thomas to survive on very little, something that would come in handy in the coming weeks. Thomas also began talking to his daughter again, and they seemed to be on the path of patching things up. She asked that he respect her decision to stay with her boyfriend, and he did so. Thomas did speak to his mother around this same time, but he was taking things with a grain of salt. A few days later, an incident occurred that would change everyone's life. While working on a roof with his friend, he received a call from his mother. He explained what he was doing and attempted to light a cigarette in the slightly windy conditions. His mother then stated, "Who is smoking pot." Thomas replied, "What are you talking about." She replied, "I can hear someone smoking pot." And he answered back, "What does smoking pot on the phone sound like cause I don't know what you're talking about." Frustrated, he hung up the phone. The following day he texted his daughter, and she replied with "Quit smoking pot." He replied, "You know I don't smoke pot, and where is this coming from?" Then he remembered his mother the day before and texted back that she was still causing issues for everyone. His mother called within minutes of that text and lit into Thomas and belittled him. It was then that Thomas, who was angry, hurt, and frustrated, cut contact off from all of them. Including his daughter, who he felt should not have been involved or put into that situation.

Thomas continued to fall deeper into depression with his mother calling on occasion, and he refused to answer. Work had come to a standstill because of heavy rain, the heaviest it had been in decades. Thomas was running out of medication, and nothing was going his way. He had job opportunities, but everything was falling through the cracks. On some nights, Thomas prayed that his life would just end. He felt he had a Guardian Angel watching over him and wondered at times if it was the Angel of Death. One night he prayed and asked for a name. Thomas drifted off to sleep and woke up shortly after a dream about an old classmate named Jon. He shrugged it off and fell back asleep. Thomas woke up again startled after hearing the name "John" shouted at him. It would be a while before he prayed to know something like that again.

Thomas started to look for ways to end his life. He began to notice repeating number sequences and finding change on the ground. Looking at the numbers, Thomas believed they were signs from above. He noticed feathers, black feathers, never seeing a white one. He thought the black feathers were and omen. Only later finding out the meaning of different colored feathers. Thomas noticed number patterns, repeating numbers which he began to research. He felt the need to get back south but was losing hope. He wrote a scathing letter to his mother, one that was brutally honest. Something he would regret down the road.

That Christmas was the darkest day he had ever faced. His daughter, the most important person in his life, was thousands of miles away. He had nothing to give her, and he was still angry and hurt that she listened to nonsense from his mother. Both Thomas and his friend felt alone that day. They cooked a meal and milled around the house.

The Journey South

By the end of January, Thomas knew he needed to get back south. There were more jobs, and he desperately needed his medication. Sitting in the local library, Thomas looked for veterans groups that would help him. Someone did, and he bought him a one-way bus ticket south. His name was John, and he did artwork. Thomas wanted to bring his cat but was not allowed to. John brought him back to the house, where he grabbed what he could, and he was off to the bus terminal. John bought him a meal and the ticket and wished him well. Thomas called his friend and tried to explain, but he was understandably upset that he had left with no explanation. But like with every other situation, Thomas's words came out a jumbled mess.

Thomas jumped on the bus, and it was headed south. Tired and nervous, he tried and failed to sleep. When the bus arrived in Atlanta, Thomas noticed a bag was missing. The bag had necessary paperwork in it, and he would never see that bag again. Thomas spent the night in the Atlanta terminal. He noticed people walking around taking pictures of other people and their bags and warned the gentleman next to him about it. They watched each other's belongings after that. That morning the journey continued, and after many stops, he reached his destination. He took a cab to the Hospital and immediately checked in with his doctor. His blood pressure was 220/107 with a slight headache, and he was exhausted. They shipped him over to the Emergency room with bags in tow. He settled in to wait his turn and noticed the people across from him. They looked familiar to him, and then he realized he had dreamt about them. It was a comfort at this point. He was brought in and was given his medication and other things to get his blood pressure under control. They kept him there for the observation that night. Thomas was released the following day and was to see his primary Doctor and a Social Worker. Thomas was homeless, and he knew he had been lost for some time, despite what his friend had said to him. He carried his bags from spot to spot, not knowing where or when he would get his next meal. He was given a bus ticket to a location to meet with a program director to see if they could help him get on his feet. He did not qualify, but a worker suggested he go to another location, and he did just that. He was accepted and given an apartment and a roommate. His roommate hooked him up with a meal that night and breakfast the following day. At times he would be thankful he had a can of chickpeas to fill his stomach until he could get to a pantry. The homeless are invisible to most people. Many drive-by ignoring what they see. Holding a sign along the That spare change helped with whatever you needed. Some needed basic everyday supplies and others to get a beer or drugs that would help them cope with whatever issue they dealt with. Thomas realized everyone had some kind of trauma they were dealing with. He made it a point that in the future, if seen someone who was holding a sign asking for help, he would do what he could. Even just lending an ear as these are people who are alcoholics and drug users and mothers who are working trying to make ends meet.

 He settled in and found it challenging to gather the paperwork he needed with many documents lost with his baggage. The coordinator of the program helped out the best that she could. He had lost his birth certificate and so much more.

Thomas started looking for work, and it was not long before he found something. He started dispatching in Medical Transportation. He submersed himself into learning a new job which was not an easy task. Not knowing the area and software was a challenge. He did not want any interference from his family as he learned the process. He missed his daughter the most but continued. Soon after, he received a call from an officer stating he was reported missing by his mother. He explained the situation and said he could not be bothered. He needed to figure things out. The officer understood and offered any assistance in the future if needed. Soon after, he received another call from the hospital to contact his daughter. He sent her a text but had no reply. A few days later, he received another call stating the same thing. This time she emailed him, and they stayed in contact. After talking for a while, he learned that things soon returned to normal for her after returning. She was doted on for a time and then felt like she was kicked to the curb. Nobody knew they were talking.

Thomas continued to excel at work, and he got along with everyone he worked with. He became the in-house tech, and a sense of security was a good feel for him. One of the issues that bothered him was that he had very little dress clothes, and he shuffled the three outfits that he did have around to make different looks until he could start picking things up at a thrift store.

By summer, he was slipping further down that black hole after his daughter asked him if he could come up for Christmas. Thomas looked at his funds and knew it was impossible. He was biking 17 miles a day to work and was caught in many downpours in the southern rains. At times his bike breaking down or the chain constantly falling off.

He was joking about steering his bike into oncoming traffic, but inside he wanted to end it. At one point, the coordinator asked what he was running from. He didn't understand himself. He would pass an area and think that would be a great spot to hang himself, then realizing he could be seen and stopped. He was smiling and laughing on the outside, but inside he was hurting. The fact was he had been hurting for years. He was preparing to end his life. Tired of all the chaos that life had thrown his way. He missed his daughter, the only genuine connection he had with anyone, and she was over a thousand miles away. He kept looking for different options and each one not being in the correct location. He continued to find black feathers on the ground and was convinced he would never find a white one. He was tired from biking so many miles a day.

He eventually found a spot where with no one to stop him. He tied two belts together off the deck rail and sat in a chair, preparing himself to end it. He pondered over all the painful moments and was relieved to know it would soon be over. But God had different plans for Thomas, for, at that moment, his daughter sent her Senior picture. He sat looking at how beautiful she was and thought. "What the fuck are you doing?" He texted her back, and they talked. He said he needed to check himself into the hospital. She asked, "Why?" Thomas replied, "Because I'm not happy and the only way I will be happy is when I'm around you." She said, "Don't say that; you're making me cry." Thomas said, "I'm sorry, honey, I'm going over and will be in touch when I can." They both said, I love you. Thomas broke down crying. Thomas made his way to the hospital with the bike in tow.

He was placed into a room with two other people in the Emergency Room. Thomas and one of them bonded as they talked. They were brought to the Psych floor and given rooms. Thomas walked into his room and immediately looked for a place to hang himself. A towel bar, a door, any spot he could find. Thomas had been looking for long that it was instilled in him. After meeting with Doctors, he told them of this.

Waiting in line for medications, he reunited with the guys from the ER. Thomas told him about losing his job because he messed up. The issues of getting away from his mother, and his daughter that he missed so much. He spoke to him and changed Thomas's thinking. It started with a simple phrase. "You locked up under a stressful situation." He told Thomas to repeat that when the negative thoughts came or when talking about it. Within a week, Thomas was doing better, and they did have some fun on the floor. Thomas bonded with another guy called Sarge, who was in a wheelchair with his right leg missing. He looked like Jack Nicholson. Thomas would push him around and help him out. On one occasion, he told him to say, "Wendy, I'm Home as he wheeled him up to the small medication window. Another time two of his friends on the floor, and Thomas were eating lunch together. Thomas listened as they talked about how circumcisions were done. Sarge had long unkempt nails and was there to be placed in assisted living. When the conversation ended, Thomas said to him, "You didn't ask the most important question?" With a puzzled look on his face, replied, "What's that?" Thomas replied, "You didn't ask him if he did the circumcision himself with those long-ass nails." Sarge looked at Thomas and flipped his middle finger up, laughing. Another guy sat next to Thomas one day and started telling him about his issues. He was nicknamed Father Mulchay from the Television show MASH. During a Church service on the floor, his friend spoke of his problems, Thomas felt compelled to do the same. Father Mulchay followed Thomas and spoke of his issues. Thomas went over to him when he was done and gave him a hug; he told him it would be alright as he sobbed. It was then that Thomas realized he wanted to do Peer Support. People could easily talk to him. Father Mulchay was a country boy, and could he sing like George Strait. Thomas encouraged him to get on a show and sing because he would have won. Thomas eventually lost contact with him.

Thomas had set it up with his Doctor that he could talk to his daughter before school. She said his sister wanted to speak with him, but he was not ready for that conversation. It was now the end of the second week, and Thomas was doing better. Doctors were talking about releasing him.

It was on a Sunday night that Thomas woke up to use the bathroom. He had spent his time Journaling and was told to write those thoughts down as they come. And as he got out of his bed, a thought came to him. It was a memory of his parents firing the babysitter after Thomas was found with a black eye. The babysitter said he fell out of the stroller. Thomas wrote this down and laid back down in bed. As he tried to go back to sleep, another thought hit him. It was a memory of his neighbor taking his temp and Thomas attempting to pull his pants down. Again he tried to sleep but was woken with another thought. At this point, he decided to stay up and go with what was coming out.

As he began to write, more and more thoughts came out, including playing Doctor as a child. He remembered going to the bathroom and grabbed toothpaste, and the problem being he knew right where to put it, using it as a lubricant. Again Thomas remembered trying to pull his pants down when playing Doctor. More and more images popped in his head. Cleaning the upstairs, making beds, and closing dresser drawers with a female voice saying, "Hurry up before your sister gets home." It was not his mother's voice. It painted a picture for him, one of sexual abuse and physical abuse, and it was then that he realized he knew too much. He broke down crying.

A doctor was brought in at 8 am, and Thomas talked about everything. The Doctor asked him.

"What would you tell little Thomas after knowing all this?" Thomas replied, "It's not his fault." As he broke down crying. He told Thomas to keep repeating this when the thoughts came. He ended up staying for another week in the hospital. He wrote his mother a letter, a different one this time. One without the anger and hurt he had written two years prior. In it, he apologized and also about the abuse. He read it to his friend and again started crying. He knew he needed to get back north to his daughter and began making plans to do so.

Thomas left the hospital and walked a couple of miles to work. Along that walk, he passed under some trees and the sun flickering between them. It was another dream Thomas remembered. He knew he was on the right path. Arriving at his job, they were glad to see him, and Thomas sat down with his boss and explained how he felt the past year and how he wanted to hang himself. She replied, "Oh my God," as he told her. He picked up his paycheck and was off to cash it and gather what he needed to head north. It was November, and he had to prepare for the cold weather. Before he left, he had to pack his things which were at his former employer. He had spent many nights sleeping there as they allowed him to do so. Putting two chairs together and resting as much as he could. While packing and talking to others and saying goodbyes to many who he considered family, he noticed that Thomas made a difference in his job. Many clients calling and asking about him and wondering where he was. This inspired him more in working with people and leaving his mark on this world. On one occasion, as he waited for the bus to take him back down to his work, he had difficulty seeing which bus he needed. He had lost contact, and everything was blurry. He tried to contact someone to pick him up, but his phone had died. He attempted to get a gentleman's attention who was walking by, and he immediately went into his pocket and was going to give him some change. Thomas replied, "No, I was going to ask you if I could use your phone to have someone pick me up." As he explained his situation. The man smiled and allowed him to do so, and Thomas thanked him. But that moment stuck with him as the man just assumed he Thomas wanted money.

A friend let him stay at his place and packed him a snack bag for the trip. As the bus headed north and made the first stop. A man on the bus approached Thomas and asked if he wanted to go with him to another state to "Help People," and of course, Thomas refused. When the bus stopped in Atlanta, he was again approached by the same man asking if he could buy him lunch. Thomas had a car close by and knew that he would not be heard from again if he went. Thomas told the man to give the money he was going to buy lunch with to the church. While at the Atlanta terminal, Thomas helped an elderly woman struggling with her bags onto the bus. They spoke before going on, and Thomas said he would sit with her after telling her what had just happened. She appreciated it, and they talked to her drop-off location.

Thomas eventually ended up at his destination 2 hours away from his hometown, and being late at night and nowhere to go, he ended up at the Hospital, and again they helped him out. He spent the night, and the following day they moved him over to a shelter.

At this point, nobody knew Thomas was back in his home state except for his daughter. He sent the letter he had written to his mother, which his uncle delivered for him. His mother replied that she understands what he was talking about with the abuse. His father and mother suspected abuse but could never put the finger on it.

His daughter was having issues with work and continued problems with her mother. She decided she would go out and party and missed the next day of work. During the next week, she would call Thomas on various nights. One evening she stated She had already "Taken 3 shots." Thomas thought it was a weeknight and with school the next day. He asked if she was at a party, and she stated she was not. She said she was alone and stressed, so she started drinking. They talked about it, and she told him she would not do that again. A few days later, she called again, saying she had smoked a joint and drove. They talked about it, and he warned her what would happen if she got pulled over or worse, got in an accident, and killed someone. As the weekend approached, she was nervous about working and started crying on the phone. Begging and pleading for help from her father. After Thomas hung up, he stared out a window and then heard a popping noise, as someone had turned on a light switch. He called everyone he could, trying to get someone to help her, and by the end of the day, he could not speak. He knew what he wanted to say, but the words would not come out of his mouth.

Thomas ended up back at the Hospital as he could not express even the simplest of thoughts. He was given a room, and for the first few days, he slept on and off. Through therapy, he regained his voice and was released just before Christmas. Thomas was placed back in the shelter and was due to have a placement in an apartment by the beginning of the New Year. He spoke with his daughter and stated, "I'm going to need your help now more than ever." She replied, "Don't worry, Dad, I love you!"

Thomas began healing and knocking down walls he had built up over the years. He found a way to say what was on his mind to people through writing. Thomas wrote his father a letter about how much those childhood moments meant to him. Things he regretted not saying to him when he was alive. But Thomas took it a step further read it out loud in private. He also wrote to those he had issues with, like the kid who bullied him back in the 2nd grade. Thomas put all his emotions into it and, at points yelling Obscenities at him but then forgiving him because he knew he had issues that he needed to deal with. Thomas did not want anything to do with him because he took in his Uncle, who had a breakdown when Thomas was in high school. He did not take great care of his Uncle, and Thomas felt that he was only in it for the money. It was soon after his Uncle passed that he quit taking people in, confirming Thomas's feelings. The more Thomas wrote and the more emotion he unleashed, a lifetime of weight was lifted off of Thomas's back. All the emotion he had held in him from childhood came out in a flood of tears. It was draining for him, but he found his voice in the process. Thomas found a way to heal himself.

While at the shelter, he started making Christmas Cookies for everyone around the holidays. Peanut Butter Blossoms, Sugar Cookies, Reindeer Cookies, to name a few. Thomas got along with everyone, more so with another guy in the building. He looked like and was built like Stone Cold Steve Austin.

He made a unique cookie just for him. A penis-shaped sugar cookie complete with blue gel for veins and black for pubic hair. A few splatters of white on the plate. He brought it into him and walked away to finish cleaning up. He walked out and smoked with his roommate who resembled a very young Ron Howard or Opie Taylor. He came out and told Thomas, "You cooked the cookie wrong." Thomas replied, "How is that?" He said, "It was so hard I couldn't bite into it." They all laughed.

He was brought to his apartment before the New Year. They stopped at a local food pantry, and he was given some food. He picked things that would last long because he didn't know how long it would be before he could return. On the 31st of December, he tried to stay awake but couldn't. While in the apartment, he started to slip again. This time it would be even worse

Walking through Hell and Back

The first few days at his apartment, he felt abandoned, and he could not complete anything that he started. He woke up in a panic at 3 am one night. In his head were the lyrics to 3 songs by Nirvana. He needed to talk to her and make sure she was alright. The lyrics made him sick to his stomach. The songs were "Something in the way," "Lake of Fire," and "Where did you sleep last night?" She was having issues with her previous boyfriend, and this caused a stir in Thomas. He could not sleep until he made contact with her. In the song "Something in the way," specific lyrics stood out. He could see a picture being painted. Her ex-boyfriend had a hard time connecting with pets, and he loved to fish.

Animals were trapped under a tarp, and it was ok to eat fish because fish don't have feelings. In the song "Where did you sleep last night he could see references to the camp where they used to go, and she had commented at one time that it was so dark because of the trees. The song references In the Pines, In the Pines, Where the sun never shines. And in the song "Lake of Fire" speaks of a lady from Duluth who was bit by a dog with a rabid tooth. Thomas remembered her brother getting bitten by a dog in the face years ago, and the lake they fished in was the lake of fire. When she called him, his first words were "Where are you?" and when she reassured him that she was home, he could breathe. What nobody knew at the time was that her ex boyfriend would cover her head with a pillow during an anxiety attack.

Over the coming weeks, Thomas slipped further and further into a black hole as things became confusing for him. Multiple stays in hospitals and doctors tried many different medications, but Thomas began to slip further and further away. Thomas wandered off at times, and his family was unable to locate him. He would find a police officer at times that would help him get to where he was going or returned safely home. They finally got him on some medications that worked, and at this point, Thomas had still not made it back to see the one person he came for, and that was his daughter. He finally made it back to his hometown, and he finally met up with her. When they finally did see each other, Thomas threw his hat off, and they hugged tightly. Both broke down in tears. Thomas told her, "I will never be that far from you again."

Thomas wanted to tell her what happened when he first went to the hospital when he was down south, but the issues with his mother led to him blurting out in front of his daughter, who broke down in tears. It resulted in another stay in the local hospital. Thomas was angry at his mother for pushing his buttons. As he waited in a room to be taken upstairs, his anger grew as nobody answered his questions as to what was going on. The anger grew more profound, and Thomas ended up firing a heavy chair into a locker along with flipping the hospital bed on its side. People amassed around him as he demanded to speak with someone and receive some answers. They complied as Thomas put the bed back in the correct position. He so badly wanted his daughter to be there with him, and she arrived a short time after. Her presence calmed him down, and he was taken to the Psych ward. While there, he wanted answers to what was going on with his mind. The Dr talked about how Thomas could not finish anything and his need for medication. This again angered Thomas as the Dr refused to listen to what Thomas was saying. Talk of schizophrenia by the Dr angered him more as Thomas told him he did not hear voices and was not delusional.

Thomas ended up leaving the hospital, and when he got back to his apartment, he weened himself off the medication. It was a short time after this that Thomas ended up speaking with the babysitter from those dark childhood days. At times, Thomas would run into an old babysitter, and they would reminisce about funny moments, but this encounter was different. They talked about those days without Thomas mentioning being abused, and her replies were very telling. Thomas mentioned being sick, and she spoke of how they would go get his sister from school. She asked if they were good memories from her time babysitting. It stuck Thomas as odd, and he replied yes, not wanting to start any confrontations. He mentioned that his parents told him she had to leave because of having seizures and how that made him sad at the time. Her only reply was, "Yeah, that was why." The conversation was very awkward, and he knew he found his answers as his stomach became knotted.

Thomas then went back to the apartment that March and was determined to find a job and get back on his feet. Within 2 weeks, he landed a job as a dispatcher/scheduler with the potential to run the company. Thomas stopped taking his medication, feeling he was over-medicated, and Thomas thought he didn't need them. Looking back, it was a regret he would have for not following through. He misread the labels, and the confusion it caused within him led him to take more than he should have. Thomas applied for food assistance, but with Covid-19 in full swing, he could not get anyone on the phone, and once he did, he was told to reapply. By that time, he was making enough to buy his food. He only worked 20hrs a week. As things began to open up, his hours increased, and he began to streamline operations by installing software for dispatching and simplifying processes. He was doing well, and he began to collect furniture for his apartment and many other things to make it feel like home. He worked a lot of hours and enjoyed working with people who had varying degrees of issues. With Covid-19 shutting down some services, it posed a challenge, but they still managed to bring in business. By September, business was slowing down, and processes were again streamlined. Thomas took a layoff and filed an unemployment claim. He took some time and headed back to his hometown to see his family. While there, Thomas found another job in transportation. And best of all, it brought him back around his daughter, who he fought so hard to get back to. With the help of his cousin, he could stay and get on his feet.

His mother continued to create problems, but Thomas understood where she came from now. She had opened up about some of the horrors she had witnessed as a child. She spoke of standing over her mother, trying to wake her up after knocked out by her father. Of having to make sure the other children were taken care of. She spoke of her Uncle who had abused her and her siblings. The same one who gave Thomas such an uneasy feeling as he watched Thomas move from room to room. Her father who would come into the bedroom at night to lift the covers and check for worms. Thomas still needed to protect himself from dealing with her issues. Ending conversations when things are spiraling out of control. At times he could get her to laugh by telling her to "Stifle it Edith" about All in the Family. Deep down, he felt sorry for her as he knew all too well what he had gone through; hers was ten times worse. It's a hell he would not wish upon anyone.

Moving forward

His job became increasingly stressful, and Thomas could not maintain the pace. His unemployment claim was still there and reopened. Again due to Covid-19, he was unable to make contact with someone regarding that claim. Messages online went unanswered.

He worked with his daughter using the tools he learned through the the hospital to help her overcome her issues. He did not want to see her going through the same thing as she had been through. He taught her the same method of Journaling and reading it out loud. And with that, things started to improve between her and her mother. And she could tell her the easiest and hardest word to say, which is "NO" She was taking control of her life. Thomas reflected over the years and realized he gave his daughter all the things he wanted but never received. Yes, she was spoiled rotten, but he gave her someone to listen to her about her problems and explain how you feel matters, the tough talks, and good ones. Thomas realized he had broken the cycle of chaos that had devastated his family for generations.

Thomas was slipping backward again as a flood of memories kept filling his mind. One, in general, was of a man yelling at him from the top of the stairs at his parent's house. Memories of being a child and being forced to wear women's lingerie. She could see him declining and became very upset, asking him to leave. Thomas went for a walk the flood gates opened. He could picture in his mind the day he dropped off his daughter, and she reached out for him yelling, "Daddy." He could still hear those cries. His life was flashing before him, all the pain and torment over the years. The last image was still playing in his mind, that of the man at the top of the stairs. It was then that the light had shown from above. Thomas again checked himself into the hospital, and when speaking to doctors, he spoke of the man and knew that was where he received the black eye as a young child. He realized his mother was trying to protect him. Thomas needed to be released from control.

Thomas was dealing with Post Traumatic Stress Disorder and Complex Trauma. The memories were flashbacks that had been coming at him for years. He had to grapple the depth of abuse he endured. Fighting the war within himself. The anger and hurt of knowing he was abused and nobody did a thing to help him. Signs and connections everywhere. Wanting a relationship with his mother and trying to suppress the feelings of no one being there for him as a child as well. It took the combined efforts of the multiple hospitals and doctors that Thomas was able to finally understand what had held him back all of these years. And for that, he was genuinely thankful to God and everyone that helped recognize this debilitating disorder. He found love, that of the unconditional love of god. Yet he still yearned for that of unconditional love in this realm. He put that in Gods loving hands. He found PTSD Therapy, which Thomas gladly accepted. Thomas aspired to work in Peer Support; he knew with what he had been through to help some people overcome some of their issues. Through the learning process of becoming a Peer Support Specialist, Thomas learned that one word would help him move forward, and that was HOPE. He knew that it was possible to recover from what is labeled Mental Illness. Peer support offered him a chance to help others that struggled. He also learned of the countless amounts of people who came off medications and going on to lead full, rich lives. Earning degrees and living with what many doctors deem uncurable. One thing that almost all people with it shared a common diagnosis in trauma. And through helping others and sharing his experiences, he could give others that same hope of living a fulfilling, successful life and not be held back from demons of the past.

While in the final few days of his stay, he reunited with someone he had not seen in 15 years. They chatted about life and what brought them there. She understood Thomas now. They became friends again and shared many laughs. And he realized how tight of a bond he had with his daughter when he spoke to her on the phone, and she stated, "Dad, I have been working hard, and you are not going to have to worry about a thing." Thomas broke down in tears when he heard this.

Thomas was heading to another facility to help him rebuild his life. He felt he could finally breathe and was ready to enjoy the rest of his life and leave those shattered days of childhood and the pain and anguish of life behind. Seven weeks of intense PTSD therapy were ahead of him, along with Dialectical Behavioral Therapy. He began moving towards the light. He could see how God had guided him on this journey, and his faith became unwavering. His daughter and her mom continued to work things out, and she found it easier to get her point across to her mother. She began to take therapy as she began to find her way. Cycles we being broken. Thomas always told her to find a job that she loves to do and use her talents in. Her goal was to become a teacher. This was a proud moment for Thomas.

Thomas learned through his classes to become a Peer Support Specialist that his diagnosis was not the end of the world. He could live a normal life and still give hope to others as he moved forward sharing his story.

Thomas made amends with his mother. He was filled with the anger of knowing that he was never helped as a child. Thomas took control of the situation and talked to his mother on his terms. He spoke of this and needing space to process this. Still she could not grasp this and he pleaded with her to get some help but it fell on deaf ears. He pleaded with her to talk to her doctor about medication. The Dr had prescribed it to her before but she refused. And by her refusal she made the decision easier for Thomas. She choose not to take the medication, just like she chose not to help Thomas when he was young. He needed to protect himself and that meant not being in his mothers life like he wanted. He would never find that acceptance from her.

Thomas from an early age, wanted to be with another family and have a different life in another town. Every family has issues like this that go back generations, and most get swept under the rug. He never was looking to blame anyone; if you need someone to blame, throw a rock in the air, you're bound to hit someone guilty. Many judge you by what they hear. Walk in his shoes, listen to what he has heard and see what he has seen. How would you handle this?

Made in the USA
Coppell, TX
07 September 2021